Countryknits II

Countryknits II

Complete patterns and instructions
for 20 casual sweaters
inspired by American folk designs

Stephen & Carol Huber

Artwork by Chesca Sheldon
Photographs of sweaters by Schecter Lee

E. P. Dutton   New York

Book design by Marilyn Rey

10 9 8 7 6 5 4 3 2 1
First Edition

CONTENTS

INTRODUCTION

Here it is!!! Our long-awaited third book of "Country" patterns. We have been absolutely delighted with the response from you, the knitters, to our first two volumes, *Countryknits* and *Countryknits for Kids*. We appreciate the fact that you started ordering the third book as soon as the second was off the press. We can hardly keep up with you!

We've had wonderful calls and letters from all over the country, and it is truly satisfying to know that you are so excited about our designs. One lady wrote to say that she has knitted almost every sweater in *Countryknits* and intends to knit all of them. Wow!

Back here on our 1685 Connecticut farm, things are busy. We are expanding quickly, trying to keep orders up to date, and creating more kits and patterns. Our little mom-and-pop operation has increased considerably with more assistance, and we have a new barn project under way to help in stocking and manufacturing kits, storing yarn and books, and giving us an office and design area. As a result, we'll be able to get out of our help's way and have a place to do more than one thing at a time, *and* we can give the barn back to the animal population. As of this writing, we have sold our cows and sheep and are down to two Briards, two cats, and our first and favorite pet—Ochipee, an aging llama. He is the one that probably started this whole thing. He was an engagement present from Steve to Carol thirteen years ago. The idea was that we would enjoy this beautiful animal: watch him grazing on the hillside, comb him out, spin the yarn, and knit gorgeous sweaters. It sounded great, but the time was never there for anything except watching him graze. Somehow we got diverted into teaching antique crafts, dealing in antiques, raising a family, and designing.

We've been thinking lately not only about the designs of our sweaters, which are gaining in popularity in the U.S. and many other countries, but also about the people who are knitting them. In this busy world with such a hectic pace, it is wonderful to know that people can still sit down and knit. Not just knitting because they have to, but because they want to. They love the art of creating beautiful designs and objects and having a useful item when they are finished. And it isn't just the older generation that is clicking needles. Young people are picking up the craft. Our daughter and head graphics person, Chesca, has taught many of her college friends to knit. They sit around their dorm rooms or crew camp and knit up a storm. Many of them are designing their own sweaters, knitting for boyfriends and parents, and all are enthusiastic about their projects.

We've had a lot of fun creating designs for sweaters. We think you'll be particularly happy with this collection. There is something for everyone: men and women, East and West, country and city.

Our Navajo Railroad and Indian Blanket designs are right out of the Southwest. The Crazy Quilt, Flower and Vine, Indiana Fan, Mosaic, and Nine Patch are classic quilt patterns from the 19th century. We've added a Reindeer adapted from a hooked rug, Smutt the famous folk-art cat, and a host of others we think you'll enjoy knitting and wearing.

Knitting has brought a lot of joy into our lives. It's a peaceful, tranquil, creative, and happy way to express oneself. We sincerely hope that we can share that with you and our patterns will bring pleasure and satisfaction to all of you who knit and wear them.

Special thanks to all of you who have helped us so much. Chesca for her unwavering support and talent; Dad and Martha for their hours of generous labor in mailing all these books; Dick, Linda, and Jane for keeping it all going; Cy, our editor, for his continual encouragement and enthusiasm; and Norma and the group of knitters in England that knit our designs into beautiful garments for prototypes and models. Thank you all!

KNITTING NOTES

ABBREVIATIONS:

alt	alternate
beg	begin(ning)
cont	continue
dec	decrease
inc	increase
K	knit
P	purl
st	stitch
st st	stockinette stitch
tog	together

TENSION OR GAUGE:

These terms are often used interchangeably. They refer to how tightly or how loosely the knitter is knitting compared with the gauge given in the pattern or by the yarn manufacturer. The gauge is the number of stitches *and* the number of rows to equal one inch. It is very important in knitting to keep this gauge correct as a mistake is multiplied with each row and the pattern will become either elongated or compressed. The horizontal gauge is the number of stitches to make one inch and determines the finished chest size. The vertical gauge is the number of rows to equal one inch and determines the finished length.

Knit a tension square before you begin any garment. Work a 2-inch square in stockinette stitch. Lay it flat and carefully measure the rows and stitches to equal one inch in each direction. If your work is larger than the specified gauge your tension is too loose and you should move down to a smaller needle. If your measurement comes out smaller, your tension is too tight and you should move to a larger needle.

DETERMINING AND ALTERING SIZE:

To determine the size garment to knit, take a chest measurement and add 2 to 4 inches depending on how tight or how loose you want the sweater to fit. (Remember, wool tends to stretch a bit.) Compare your tension with the gauge and make any needle corrections. Take measurements for the following: length of finished garment from underarm, length of finished garment from middle of shoulder, and length of finished sleeve to underarm. Compare your measurements with those given for the pattern and lengthen or shorten as needed.

SIZING:

(1) Measure chest. (2) Add 2 to 4 inches (depending on how loose you want the sweater). (3) Divide total measurement by 2. (4) Multiply this number by the number of sts in one inch. This gives the number of sts needed for front and back. (5) Subtract 8 from above number for ribbing. (6) Cast on number of sts from step 5. Work in ribbing for K1, P1 for 3 inches and increase 8 sts in next row using st st. (7) Follow graph, deleting or adding pattern from graph at sides. Work to underarm. (8) Measure from underarm to desired length. (9) Subtract 3 inches (ribbing). (10) Multiply by number of rows per inch. This gives the number of rows for desired underarm length. (11) Adjust graph by adding or deleting as necessary. (12) Measure desired length to neck edge of shoulder. (13) Subtract underarm length. (14) Multiply by the number of rows per inch. This gives the number of rows for desired length from underarm to shoulder. (Allow a little extra for sufficient arm movement.) (15) Unless you are knitting a very large (44″ and over), or very small (34″ and under) garment, the neck will not need adjustment. However, sts can be added or deleted and neck edge moved in or out. (16) Shoulders will have the number of sts determined by the number cast on at beginning. At underarm bind off according to chart and follow decreasing. (17) At shoulder divide total number of sts on each side by 3. Bind off as pattern shows. (18) Measure length of sleeve to underarm. (19) Subtract 3 inches for ribbing. (20) Multiply by the number of rows

per inch. Adjust pattern by adding or deleting rows. (21) Follow pattern for top of shoulder. (22) For small sizes (34″ and under) delete 2 to 3 sts each side of sleeve pattern. For large sizes (44″ and over) add 2 to 3 sts each side of sleeve pattern.

An alternative method of adjusting the size is too increase the size of the garment by using bulkier yarns or to decrease the size of the sweater by using finer yarns. The yarn-gauge charts show many different yarns, a needle number, and the number of stitches per inch and the number of rows per inch. Check your gauge with the graph to determine the size garment you will end up with by following the charted graph with a different yarn.

GRAPHS:

The patterns in this book are all charted on graphs. Each square represents one stitch. The patterns are shown in color, or in black and white. The black-and-white have different symbols to distinguish the colors. Adjustments can be made by adding or deleting rows, or moving the side seam and armhole line in or out. Increase and decrease stitches are indicated on the sides, and binding off is designated by decreasing more than one stitch.

YARN-GAUGE CHARTS:

The yarn-gauge charts are included so that one can quickly convert a pattern from one type of yarn to another. Heavy-weight wools can be used for sweaters calling for sport-weight yarn, or vice versa, by adjusting the pattern according to the above directions and using the yarn-gauge charts as a guide to needle size and tension. It's fun; by all means experiment!

KNITTING THE GARMENT:

Here are a few general notes on the actual knitting of the sweater. For a neater edge, whenever possible slip the first stitch and knit into the back of the last stitch on every row. This will create a neater edge, and it will be easier to sew and match up the pattern.

Do not join yarn in the middle of a row; it usually shows and creates a bulky area. Join at the beginning of the row with a new ball and use both ends for sewing seams later.

An especially important note about the sweater patterns in this book. Do not carry the yarn across the back of the sweater when working pattern motifs. Use bobbins (or small balls) and change yarn with each color change simply by looping the first yarn around the new color and continuing with the new yarn. This is very important with heavy yarns as they tend to pucker and become bulky.

SEWING TOGETHER:

To join the garment together, use the same yarn it was knitted with. Use a running stitch and go through each stitch on each side of the seam. (A back stitch makes the seam bulky, and an overcast stitch is not as neat.) Make sure not to pull the yarn too tightly and secure the ends of the seam with a double stitch. Weave in all ends 2 or 3 inches before cutting. Do not knot sewing yarns.

BLOCKING:

Wool and cotton sweaters should be pressed when completed so that the seams will lie flat. When blocking, use a damp cloth and a warm iron. Lay the seams flat and press down with the iron but do not go back and forth. Wool tends to mat and become shiny if pressed too long. It is easier to sew the shoulder and sleeve/armhole seams first and then press before sewing the long sleeve and side seam.

WASHING:

Hand-knitted garments should be hand-washed. Use a mild detergent and lukewarm water. Do not rub, wring, twist, scrub, or let the water run directly on the garment. Gently push the sweater into the water and lightly agitate it up and down. Do not soak for long as this mats wool. Rinse thoroughly, squeeze slightly, and roll between two towels to remove excess water. Lay flat and smooth back into shape.

YARN-GAUGE CHART

Group A Yarns	Needle Size	Gauge
George Picaud Lambswool	5	7 sts 8½ rows
Columbia-Minerva Scotch Fingering	4	7 sts 9 rows
Columbia-Minerva Nantuck Fingering	4	7 sts 9 rows

Group B Yarns	Needle Size	Gauge
Columbia-Minerva Featherweight Knitting Worsted	5	6 sts 7½ rows
Columbia-Minerva Shetland Wool	5	6 sts 7½ rows
Bernat Berella Sportspun	5	6 sts 8 rows
Picaud Laine et Coton	5	6 sts 8 rows
Chat Botte Petrouchka	4	6 sts 8 rows
3 Suisses Suizy DK	5	6 sts 6½ rows
Patons Clansman DK	4	6½ sts 7½ rows
S. & C. Huber's American Classic 100% cotton	5	6 sts 6½ rows

Group C Yarns	Needle Size	Gauge
S. & C. Huber's American Classic 100% wool, Fisherman 2-ply	6	5 sts 6½ rows
Galler's Olympic-Supra 100% wool	8	5 sts 6 rows
Unger Natuurwol	6	5 sts 6 rows
Pingouin Comfortable Sport	6	5 sts 6½ rows
Galler's Cotton Express	6	5 sts 6 rows
Galler's Parisian Cotton RBC	6	5 sts 6 rows
Columbia-Minerva Nantuck Sports	6	5 sts 7 rows
Bernat Sesame 4	8	5 sts 7 rows
Bernat Berella "4"	8	5 sts 7 rows
Galler's Pony, 100% cotton	5	5½ sts 6½ rows
Unger's Britania	6	5½ sts 7 rows
Lister-Lee Motoravia DK	5	5½ sts 8 rows
Phildar Sagittaire	4	5½ sts 8 rows

Group D Yarns	Needle Size	Gauge
Sunbeam Aran	7	4½ sts 6 rows
Columbia-Minerva Knitting Worsted	8	4½ sts 6 rows
Columbia-Minerva Heatherglo	8	4½ sts 6 rows
Nantuck 4-ply Knitting Worsted	8	4½ sts 6 rows
Nantuck Dimension	8	4½ sts 6 rows
Nantuck Spectra	8	4½ sts 6 rows
Reverie	8	4½ sts 6 rows

SIZE CHART
(Number of stitches needed for the front or the back)

Finished Size	34	36	38	40	42	44
Group A Yarns	119	126	133	140	147	154
Group B Yarns	102	108	114	120	126	132
Group C Yarns	85	90	95	100	105	110
Group D Yarns	76	81	86	90	94	99

NEEDLE CONVERSION CHART

Metric U.K. & Australia	U.K., Australia Canada, S. Africa	U.S.A.
2	14	00
2¼	13	0
2¾	12	1
3	11	2
3¼	10	3
3¾	9	4
4	8	5
4½	7	6
5	6	7
5½	5	8
6	4	9
6½	3	10
7	2	10½
7½	1	11
8	0	12
9	00	13
10	000	15

SMUTT-THE-CAT CREW-NECK PULLOVER

And what a cat he is! Probably the most famous of all folk-art cats, Smutt is a gorgeous tiger that graces calendars and books. Painted in the 19th century, he looks just as good when he's knitted as he does on canvas.

MATERIALS: 20 oz. background in sport-weight wool, cotton, or yarn to give gauge below. 2 oz. each of two different colors for cat, 1 oz. mohair for cat's chest, 2 oz. color for rug, 1 oz. each of two different colors for flowers, 1 oz. green, small amount dark brown for eyes.

NEEDLES: Size 4 and 6. One set of double-point needles size 4.

GAUGE: 5½ sts = 1 inch. 6½ rows = 1 inch. Correct needle size if necessary.

SIZE: These directions are for a size 39″ finished garment using inside lines. Measurements are: length to underarm 18″, length to shoulder 25″, length of sleeve to underarm 19″.

For size 42″ use outside lines and larger neck opening. Enlarge sleeve by 3 sts on each side.

To alter size, see instructions for SIZING. An oversize sweater can be made using this pattern with worsted weight wool and size 5 and 7 needles.

NOTE: Do *NOT* carry yarn across. Use a new yarn for each color change and twist old and new yarns around each other to prevent holes.

FRONT: With size 4 needles, cast on 96 sts. Work in K1, P1, ribbing for 3 inches. Change to size 6 needles and increase 12 sts evenly spaced on next row working in st st. Continue in st st and work charted design, binding off and decreasing as indicated. Place the 24 sts in center of front on holder to be picked up later for neck ribbing.

BACK: Work to match front. Place 35 sts in center of back on holder for neck ribbing.

SLEEVES: With size 4 needles, cast on 42 sts. Work in K1, P1, ribbing for 3 inches. Change to size 6 needles and increase 6 sts evenly spaced in next row using st st. Work sleeves according to charted design.

Sew shoulder seams.

NECK: With size 4 double-point needles and right side facing, pick up and K across 35 sts on back holder, pick up and K 15 sts to front holder, K across 24 sts on front holder, and pick up and K 16 sts to back. Total 90 sts. K1, P1, in ribbing for 1 inch. Bind off loosely in ribbing.

Sew sleeves in place. Sew underarm and sleeve seams. Weave in loose threads.

Smutt-the-Cat
Crew-Neck Pullover

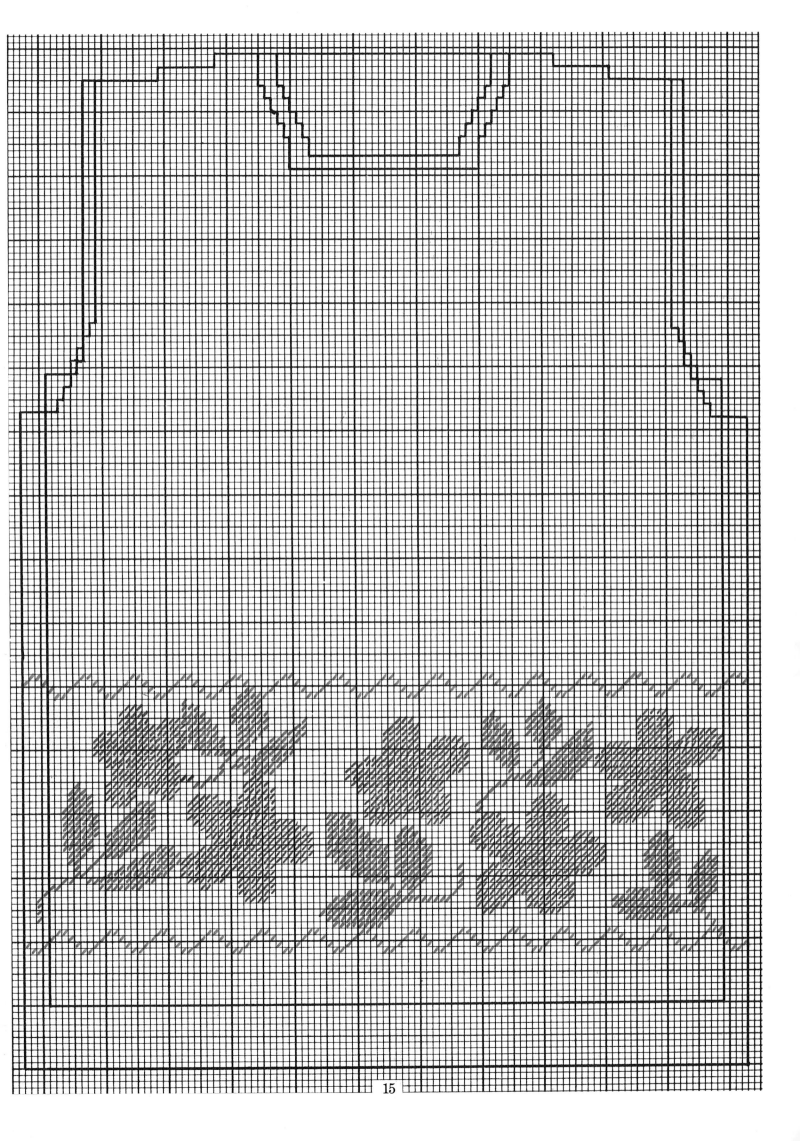

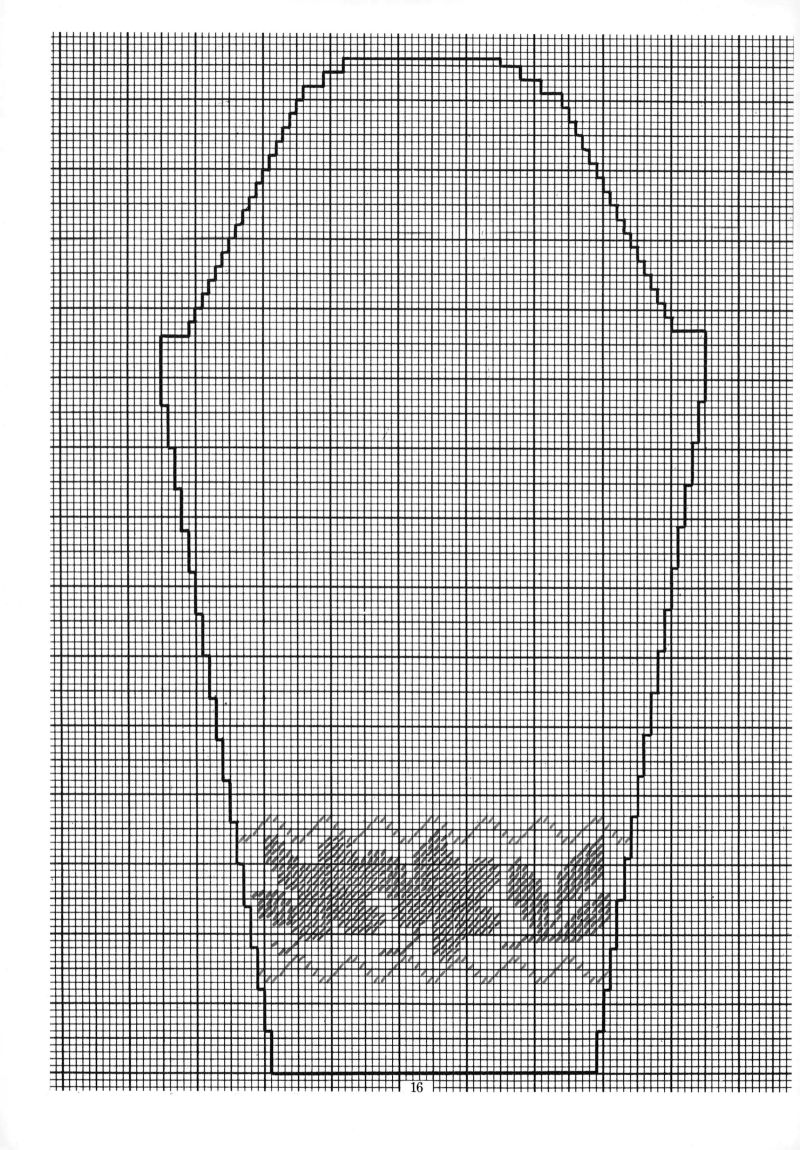

Crazy Quilt
Crew-Neck Pullover

CRAZY QUILT CREW-NECK PULLOVER

The Crazy Quilt pattern is quick and creative, a great way to use up tidbits of yarn. The sweater, inspired by a 19th-century quilt, has black sleeves and patches of black over the front and back, filled in with a multitude of different colors and embroidered squares. For a really special effect, outline each block in yellow yarn after knitting, using a variety of stitches — blanket, cross, running, etc. This was a typical method of embellishing a Crazy quilt.

MATERIALS: 12 to 14 oz. main color (usually black) in sport-weight wool, cotton, or yarn to give gauge below. 1 to 2 oz. of six to seven different colors. Victorians liked dark shades — black, brown, tan, cranberry, dark green, blue, lavender, etc.

NEEDLES: Size 4 and 6. One set of double-point needles size 4.

GAUGE: 5½ sts = 1 inch. 6½ rows = 1 inch. Correct needle size if necessary.

SIZE: These directions are for a size 39″ finished garment using inside lines. Measurements are: length to underarm 18″, length to shoulder 25″, length of sleeve to underarm 19″.

For size 42″ use outside lines and larger neck opening. Enlarge sleeve by 3 sts on each side.

To alter size, see instructions for SIZING. An oversize sweater can be made using this pattern with worsted weight wool and size 5 and 7 needles.

NOTE: Do *NOT* carry yarn across. Use a new yarn for each color change and twist old and new yarns around each other to prevent holes.

FRONT: With size 4 needles, cast on 96 sts. Work in K1, P1, ribbing for 3 inches. Change to size 6 needles and increase 12 sts evenly spaced on next row working in st st. Continue in st st and work charted design, using colors of choice in various blocks, binding off and decreasing as indicated. Place the 24 sts in center of front on holder to be picked up later for neck ribbing.

BACK: Work to match front. Fill in pattern at neck to shoulders and place 35 sts in center of back on holder for neck ribbing.

SLEEVES: With size 4 needles, cast on 42 sts. Work in K1, P1, ribbing for 3 inches. Change to size 6 needles and increase 6 sts evenly spaced in next row using st st. Work sleeves according to charted design.

Sew shoulder seams.

NECK: With size 4 double-point needles and right side facing, pick up and K across 35 sts on back holder, pick up and K 15 sts to front holder, K across 24 sts on front holder, and pick up and K 16 sts to back. Total 90 sts. K1, P1, in ribbing for 1 inch. Bind off loosely in ribbing.

Sew sleeves in place. Sew underarm and sleeve seams. Weave in loose threads. Swiss darn motifs in patches.

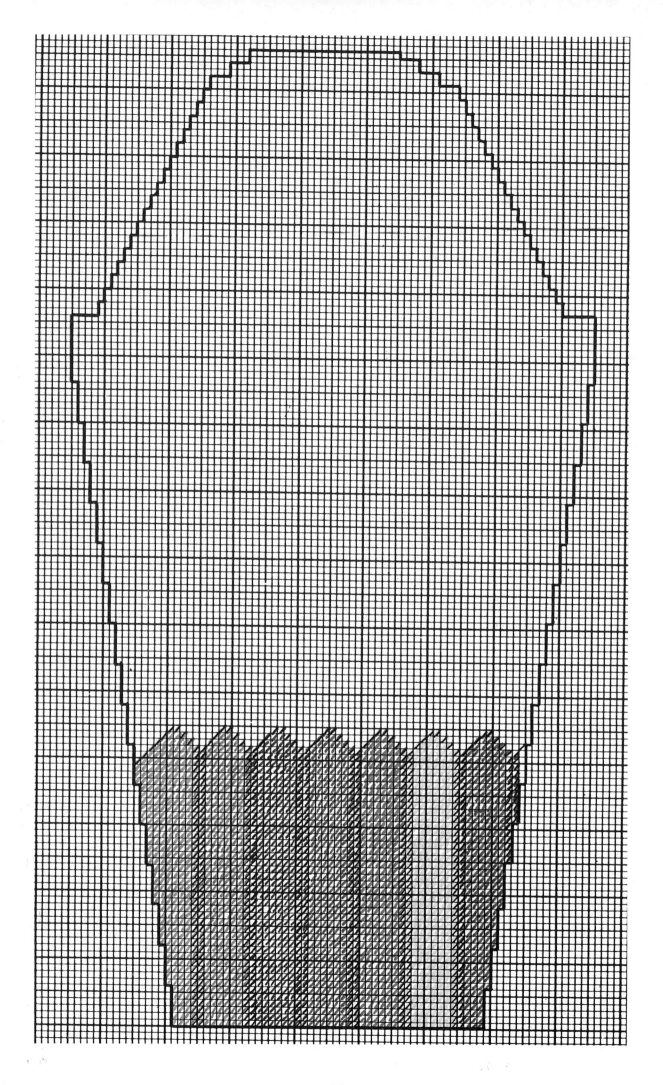

Indian Blanket
Crew-Neck Pullover

INDIAN BLANKET CREW-NECK PULLOVER

This variation on an Indian blanket design appears to be a forerunner to Op art. It's great for men or women and you can use your imagination with the placement of colors.

MATERIALS: 14 to 16 oz. of background color in yarn to give gauge below. 2 to 4 oz. of six to eight different colors.

NEEDLES: Size 4 and 7. One set of double-point needles size 4.

GAUGE: 5 sts = 1 inch. 6½ rows = 1 inch.

SIZE: These directions are for a size 40″ finished garment. Measurements are: length to underarm 16″, length to shoulder 24½″, length of sleeve to underarm 18″.

To alter size, see instructions for SIZING.

NOTE: Do *NOT* carry yarn across. Use a separate yarn for each color change and twist old and new yarn around each other to prevent holes. Loose ends are woven in later.

FRONT: With size 4 needles and main color, cast on 80 sts. Work in K1, P1, ribbing for 3 inches. Change to size 7 needles and increase 20 sts in next row working in st st. Continue in st st and work charted design, binding off and decreasing as indicated. Place center 16 sts on holder for neck ribbing.

BACK: Work to match front. Fill in pattern at neck to shoulders and place 36 sts in center of back on holder for neck ribbing.

SLEEVES: With size 4 needles, cast on 34 sts. Work in K1, P1, ribbing for 3 inches. Change to size 7 needles and increase 10 sts on next row, evenly spaced working in st st. Work sleeves according to charted design, measuring length as work is done to correct length.

Sew shoulder seams.

NECK: With size 4 double-point needles and right side facing, pick up and K across 36 sts on back holder, pick up and K 14 sts to front holder, K across 16 sts on front holder, and pick up and K 14 sts to back. Total 80 sts. K1, P1, in ribbing for 1 inch. Bind off loosely in ribbing.

Sew sleeves in place, as marked on pattern. Sew underarm and sleeve seams. Weave in loose threads.

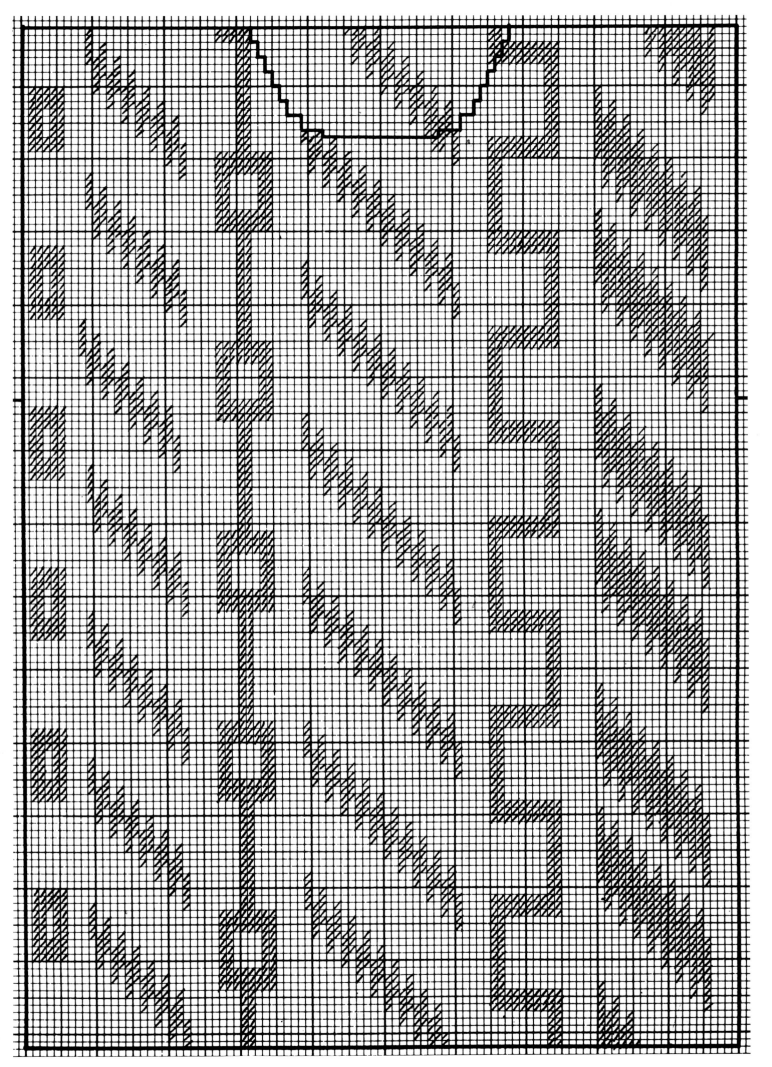

23

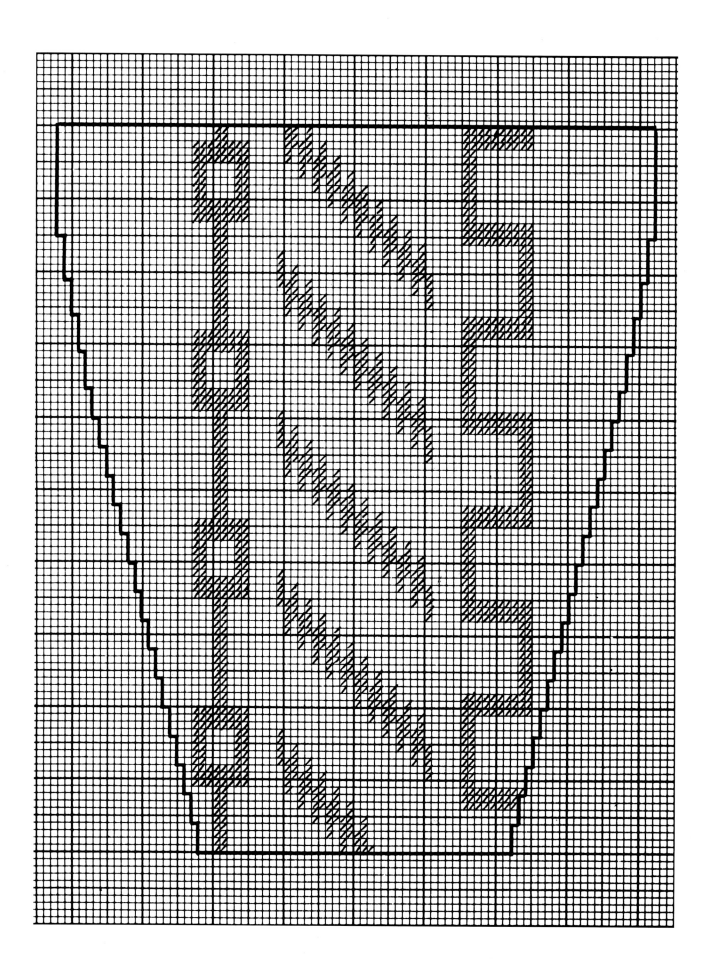

Hearts and Hands
Crew-Neck Pullover

HEARTS AND HANDS CREW-NECK PULLOVER

A popular 19th-century motif, hearts and hands were used decoratively on valentines, sketches, wooden items, and needlework. We've made this happy design into a long tunic-style sweater. Should you want a standard length, just omit one or two of the bands.

MATERIALS: 24-26 oz. background color in knitting worsted weight or yarn to give recommended gauge below. 4 oz. red, 4 oz. yellow, 4 oz. blue, 3 oz. green.

NEEDLES: Size 4 and 6. One set of double-point needles size 4.

GAUGE: 5 sts = 1 inch. 6½ rows = 1 inch.

SIZE: These directions are for a size 43" finished garment. Measurements are: length to underarm 22½", length to shoulder 29½", length of sleeve to underarm 19".

NOTE: Do *NOT* carry yarn across. Use a new yarn for each color change and twist old and new yarns around each other to prevent holes.

FRONT: With size 4 needles, cast on 98 sts. Work in K1, P1, ribbing for 2½ inches. Change to size 6 needles and increase 10 sts evenly spaced across next row working in st st. Continue in st st and work charted design, binding off and decreasing as indicated. Place the center 24 sts on holder for neck ribbing.

BACK: Work to match front. Place the center 34 sts on holder for neck ribbing.

SLEEVES: With size 4 needles, cast on 42 sts. Work in K1, P1, ribbing for 3 inches. Change to size 6 needles and increase 6 sts evenly spaced in next row working in st st. Work sleeves according to charted design, increasing and decreasing as indicated.

Sew shoulder seams.

NECK: With size 4 double-point needles and right side facing, pick up and K across 34 sts on back holder, pick up and K 15 sts to front holder, K across 24 sts on front holder, and pick up and K 15 sts to back. Total 88 sts. K1, P1, in ribbing for 1 inch. Bind off loosely in ribbing.

Sew sleeves in place. Sew underarm and sleeve seams. Weave in loose threads.

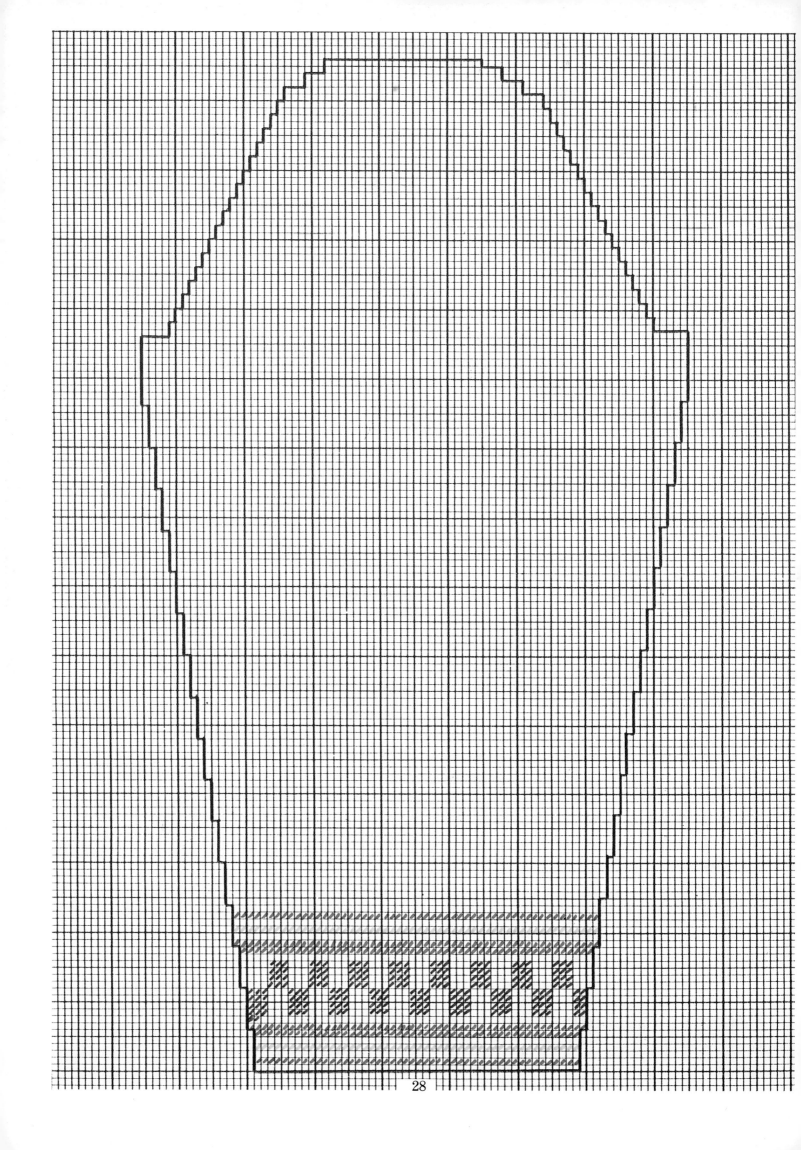

Mosaic Quilt
Crew-Neck Pullover

MOSAIC QUILT CREW-NECK PULLOVER

One of Granny's favorites, this works up into a terrific sweater. Colors can be combined in any fashion, repeated or random. A great way to use up yarn leftovers, just like the 19th-century woman used fabric scraps in her quilts.

MATERIALS: 14 to 16 oz. of background or main color in knitting worsted weight wool, cotton, or yarn to give gauge below. 2 to 4 oz. of six to eight different colors.

NEEDLES: Size 4 and 7. One set of double-point needles size 4.

GAUGE: 4½ sts = 1 inch. 6½ rows = 1 inch. Correct needle size if necessary.

SIZE: These directions are for a size 44″ finished garment. Measurements are: length to underarm 16½″, length to shoulder 24½″, length of sleeve to underarm 18″.

To alter size, see instructions for SIZING.

NOTE: Do *NOT* carry yarn across. Use a separate yarn for each color change and twist old and new yarn around each other to prevent holes. Loose ends are woven in later.

FRONT: With size 4 needles and main color, cast on 80 sts. Work in K1, P1, ribbing for 3 inches. Change to size 7 needles and increase 20 sts in next row working in st st. Continue in st st and work charted design, binding off and decreasing as indicated. Place center 16 sts on holder for neck ribbing.

BACK: Work to match front. Fill in pattern at neck to shoulders and place 36 sts in center of back on holder for neck ribbing.

SLEEVES: With size 4 needles, cast on 34 sts. Work in K1, P1, ribbing for 3 inches. Change to size 7 needles and increase 10 sts on next row, evenly spaced working in st st. Work sleeves according to charted design, measuring length as work is done to correct length.

Sew shoulder seams.

NECK: With size 4 double-point needles and right side facing, pick up and K across 36 sts on back holder, pick up and K 14 sts to front holder, K across 16 sts on front holder, and pick up and K 14 sts to back. Total 80 sts. K1, P1, in ribbing for 1 inch. Bind off loosely in ribbing.

Sew sleeves in place, as marked on pattern. Sew underarm and sleeve seams. Weave in loose threads.

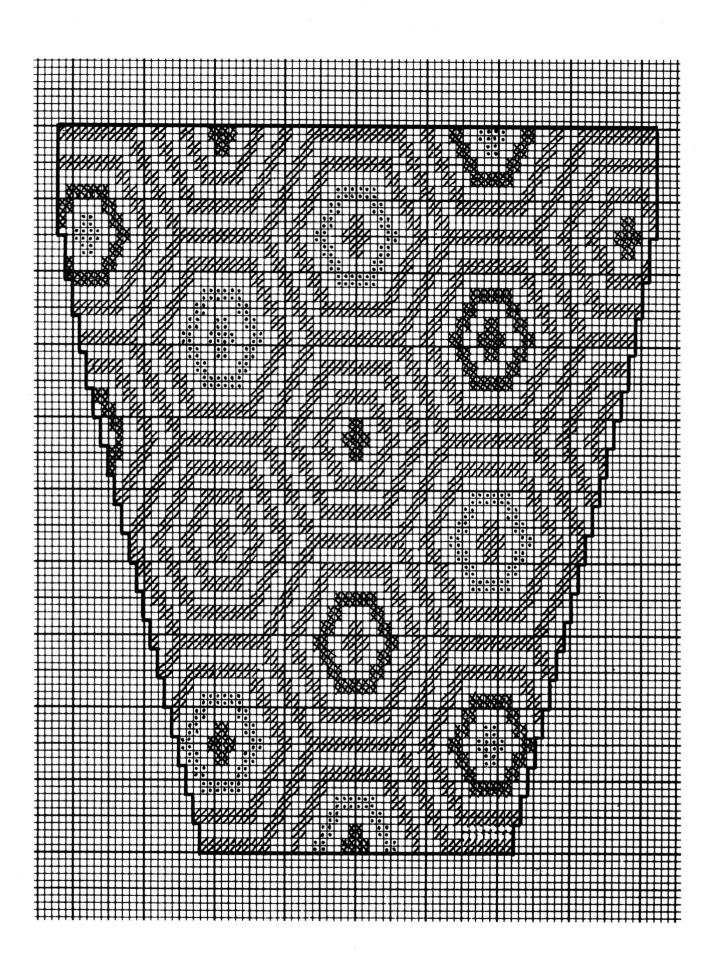

Pig-on-a-Blanket
Crew-Neck Pullover

PIG-ON-A-BLANKET CREW-NECK PULLOVER

Our pig, a fat little porker, comes from the central motif of a hooked rug. He looks great in any color combination. The flowering vine, derived from a quilt, continues around the back and sleeves for a nice decorative accent.

MATERIALS: 20 oz. knitting worsted or yarn to give recommended gauge below. 4 oz. pink, 4 oz. red, 2 oz. light blue, 2 oz. green, 1 oz. tan.

NEEDLES: Size 4 and 7. One set of double-point needles size 4.

GAUGE: 4½ sts = 1 inch. 6½ rows = 1 inch. Correct needle size if necessary.

SIZE: These directions are for a size 44″ finished garment. Measurements are: length to underarm 16½″, length to shoulder 24½″, length of sleeve to underarm 18″.

To alter size, see instructions for SIZING.

NOTE: This is a drop shoulder and does not hit at the usual shoulder seam. Check sleeves for length while knitting.

FRONT: With main color and size 4 needles, cast on 84 sts and work in K1, P1, ribbing for 2 inches. Increase 16 sts evenly spaced across next row of ribbing. Change to larger needles and working in st st follow graphed design. Increase, decrease, and bind off as indicated. Place center sts of neck on holder for neck ribbing.

BACK: Work as for front, omitting central motif, but continuing borders.

SLEEVES: With smaller needles and main color cast on 34 sts. Work in K1, P1, ribbing for 2 inches. Increase 10 sts in next row of ribbing, 44 sts. Change to larger needles and work in st st following charted design. Increase and bind off as indicated.

Sew shoulder seams.

NECK: With right sides facing and double-point needles, begin at right shoulder, pick up and K 36 sts along back neck, 44 sts along front neck — 80 sts. Work in K1, P1, ribbing for 1 inch. Bind off loosely in ribbing.

Sew sleeves in front and back. Sew sleeve and side seams.

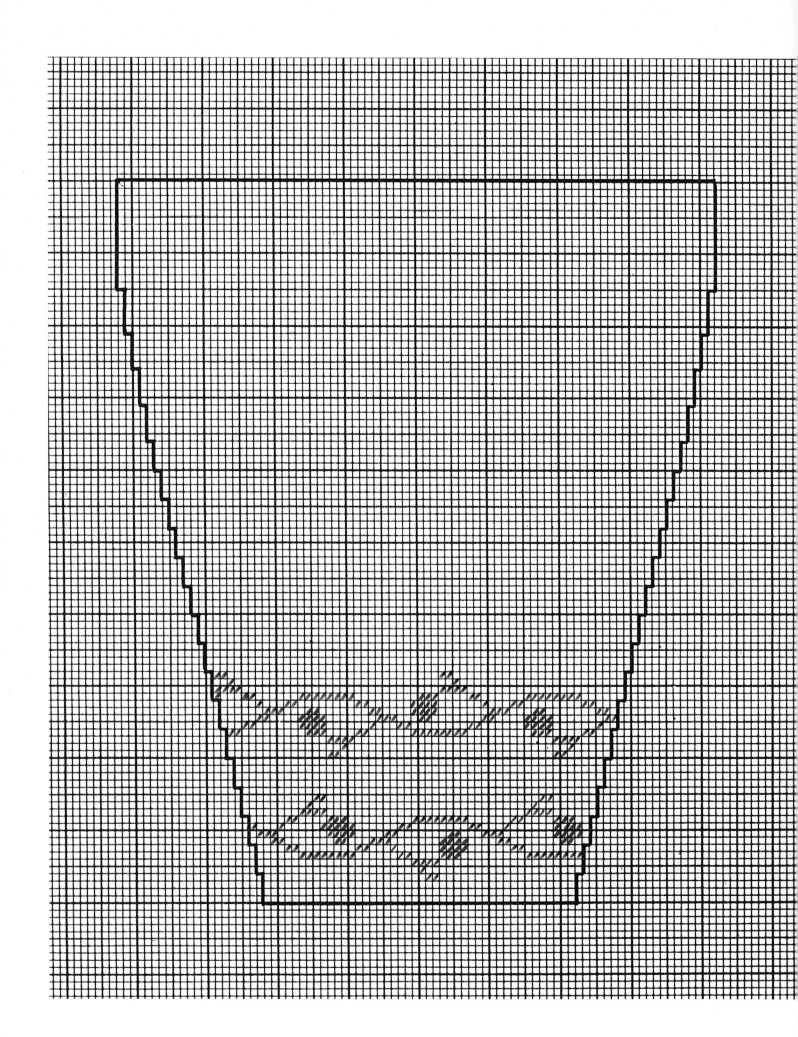

Diamond with Flower
Crew-Neck Pullover

DIAMOND WITH FLOWER CREW-NECK PULLOVER

Adapted from a crewel-embroidered bedcover, this delightful diamond pattern is quickly knit, and the flowers are worked later in duplicate stitch. For a razzle-dazzle effect, work the diamonds in different colors.

MATERIALS: 20-22 oz. main color in knitting worsted or yarn to give recommended gauge below. 4 oz. white for diamonds, 2 oz. red, and 2 oz. green.

NEEDLES: Size 4 and 7. One set of double-point needles, size 4.

GAUGE: 4½ sts = 1 inch. 6½ rows = 1 inch.

SIZE: These directions are for a size 39″ finished garment. Measurements are as follows: length to underarm 15¾″, length to shoulder 25″, length of sleeve to underarm 18″.

To alter size see instructions for SIZING.

FRONT: With size 4 needles, cast on 80 sts. Work in K1, P1, ribbing for 3 inches. Change to size 7 needles and increase 8 sts evenly spaced on next row working in st st. Continue in st st and work the charted design, binding off and decreasing as indicated. Place the 14 sts in center of front on holder to be picked up later for neck ribbing.

BACK: Work back to match front. Fill in pattern at neck to shoulders and place 26 sts in center of back on holder for neck ribbing.

SLEEVES: Cast on 40 sts on size 4 needles. Work in K1, P1, ribbing for 3 inches. Change to size 7 needles and increase 8 sts evenly spaced in next row using st st. Work sleeves according to charted design.

Sew shoulder seams.

NECK: With size 4 double-point needles, K across sts on back holder with right side facing. Pick up and K 56 sts to right shoulder (including sts on front holder). K1, P1, in ribbing on 82 sts for 1 inch. Bind off loosely in ribbing.

Sew sleeves in place. Sew underarm and sleeve seams. Swiss darn flowers in squares. Weave in loose threads.

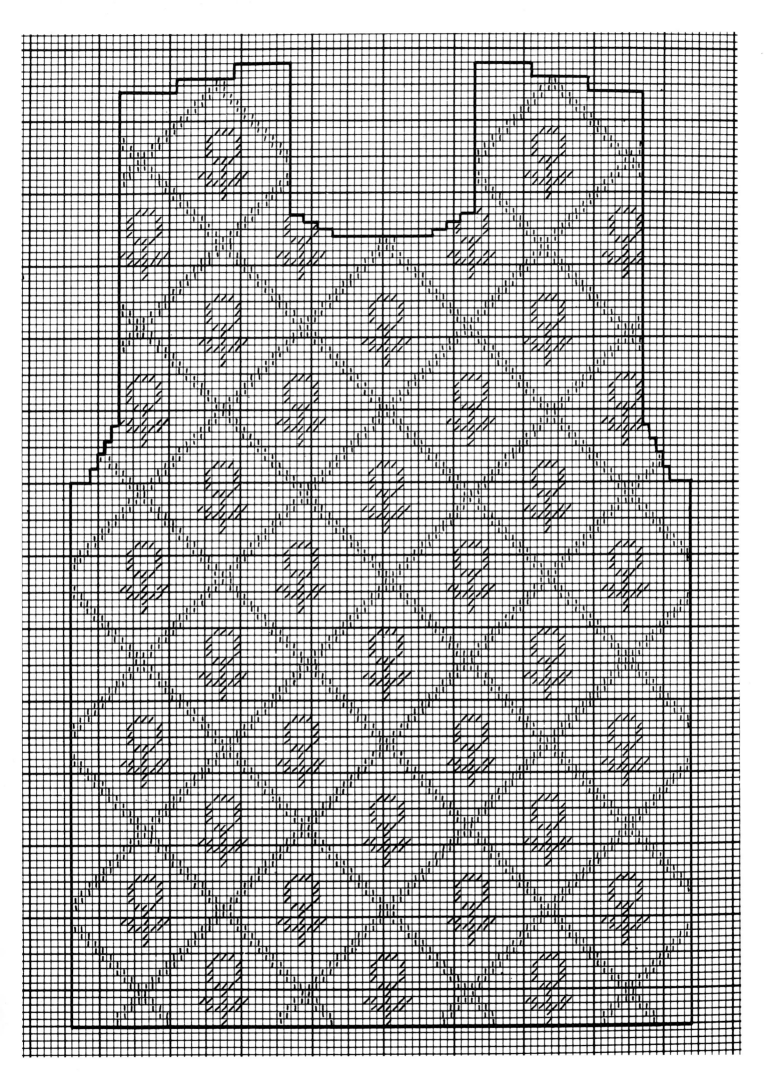

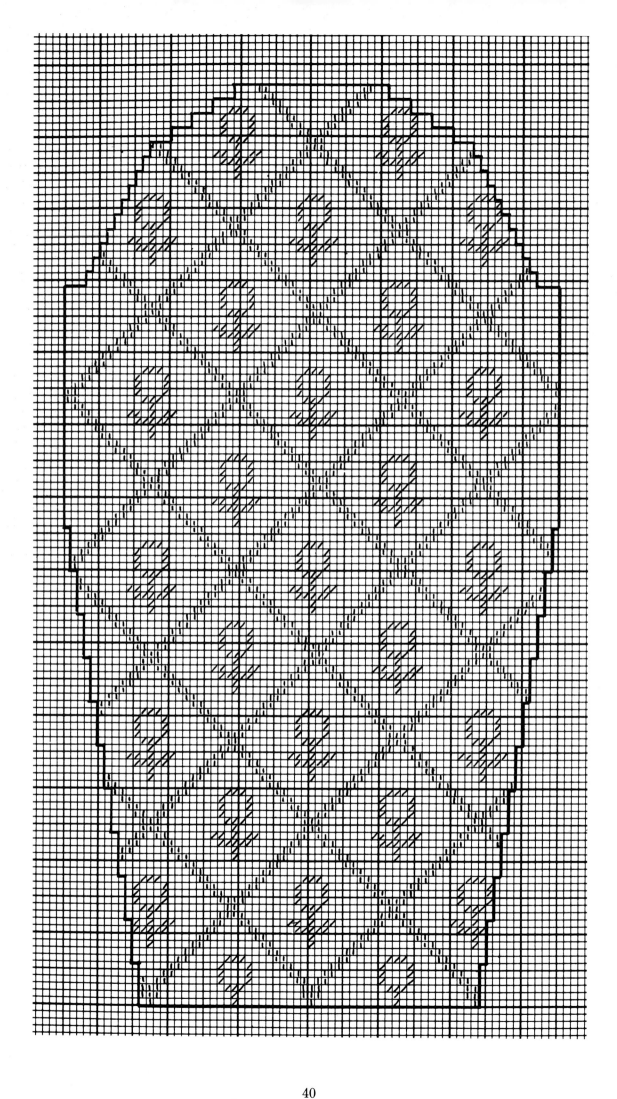

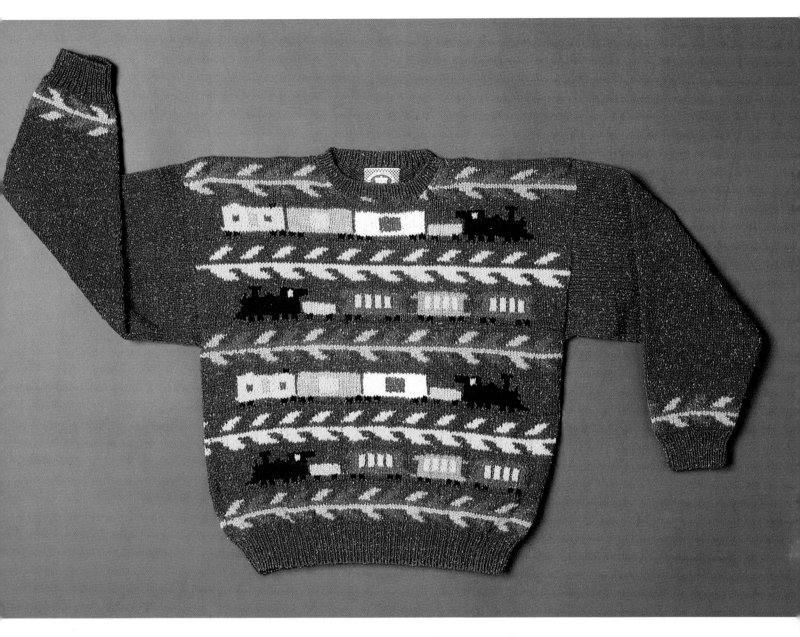

Navajo Railroad
Crew-Neck Pullover

NAVAJO RAILROAD CREW-NECK PULLOVER

This colorful train sweater is an adaptation of a Navajo blanket woven around 1890. A major event in the history of America's Southwest, the trains look just as great in a sweater as they do in a blanket. Suitable for both men and women, this is fun to knit and exciting to wear.

MATERIALS: 16 to 18 oz. background color, in sport-weight wool, cotton, or yarn to give gauge below. 2 oz. each of gold, dark blue, green, and black. ½ oz. each of white, brown, tan, and light blue.

NEEDLES: Size 4 and 6. One set of double-point needles size 3.

GAUGE: 5 sts = 1 inch. 6½ rows = 1 inch. Correct needle size if necessary.

SIZE: These directions are for a size 43″ finished garment. Measurements are: length to underarm 18″, length to shoulder 25½″, length of sleeve to underarm 20″.

To alter size, see instructions for SIZING.

NOTE: Do *NOT* carry yarn across back. Use a new yarn for each color change and twist old and new yarns around each other to prevent holes.

FRONT: With size 4 needles and main color, cast on 92 sts. Work in K1, P1, ribbing for 2½ inches. Change to size 6 needles and increase 16 sts evenly spaced on next row working in st st. Continue in st st and work the charted design, following color key and binding off and decreasing as indicated. Place the 23 sts in center front on holder to be picked up later for neck ribbing.

BACK: Work to match front. Place 39 sts in center of back on holder for neck ribbing.

SLEEVES: With size 4 needles, cast on 48 sts. Work in K1, P1, ribbing for 2½ inches. Change to size 6 needles and increase 9 sts evenly spaced in next row using st st. Work sleeves according to charted design, measuring length desired as worked.

Sew shoulder seams.

NECK: With size 4 double-point needles and right side facing, pick up and K across 39 sts on back holder, pick up and K 14 sts to front holder, K across 23 sts on front holder, and pick up and K 14 sts to back. Total 90 sts. K1, P1, in ribbing for 1 inch. Bind off loosely in ribbing.

Sew sleeves in place, as marked on pattern. Sew underarm and sleeve seams. Weave in loose threads.

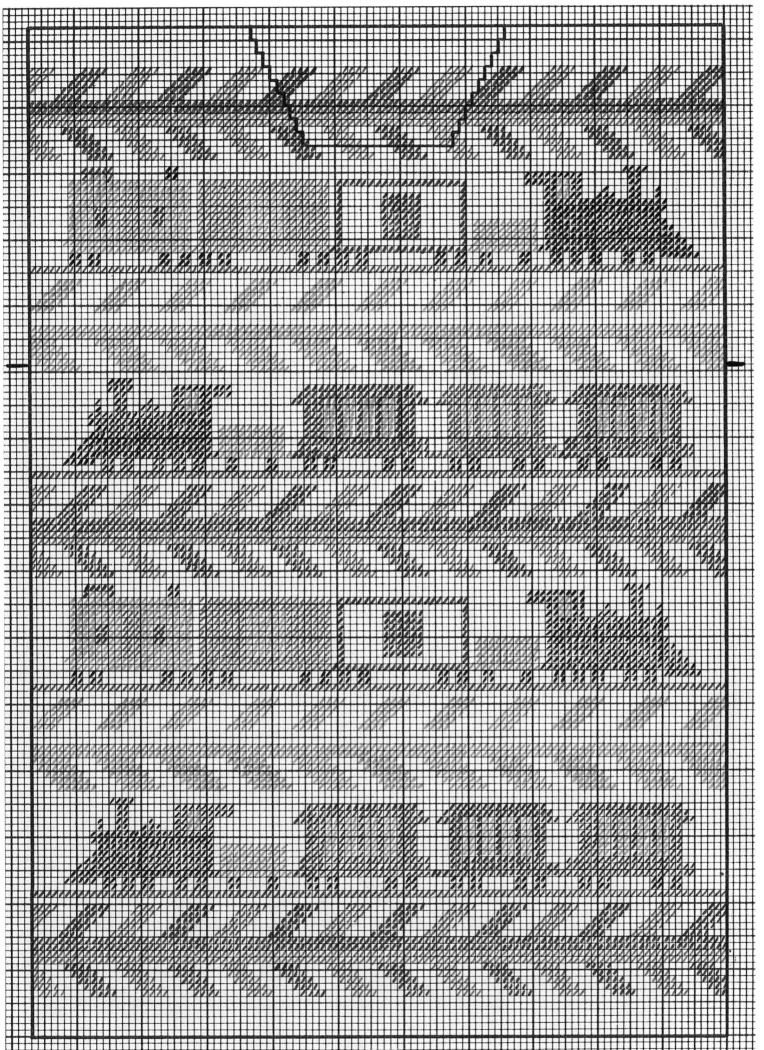

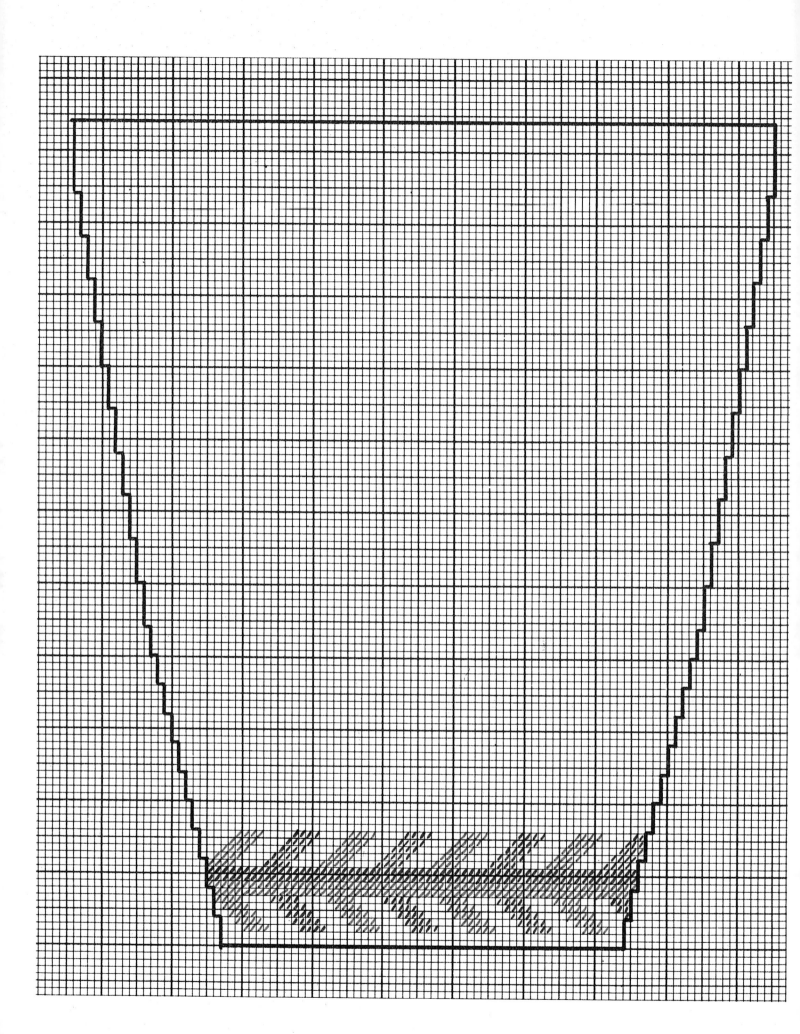

Indiana Fan
Crew-Neck Pullover

INDIANA FAN CREW-NECK PULLOVER

A wild, late 19th-century quilt design, this almost looks like an example of American Pop art. The original had squares with a variety of dark backgrounds behind the zig-zag, but we think it's just as effective to have the fans dancing across a solid ground. It's fun and very "in."

MATERIALS: 12-15 oz. of dark background color (1 dark shade or several) in sport-weight wool, cotton, or yarn to give recommended gauge below. 2-3 oz. of six to eight different colors.

NEEDLES: Size 4 and 6. One set of double-point needles, size 4.

GAUGE: 5½ sts = 1 inch, 7 rows = 1 inch.

SIZE: These directions are for a size 39″ finished garment. Measurements are: length to underarm 20″, length to shoulder 28″, length of sleeve to underarm 18″. This is a long pattern and rows should be deleted where necessary to insure correct fit.

To alter size see instructions for SIZING.

NOTE: Do *NOT* carry yarn across. Use a new yarn for each color change and twist old and new yarns around each other to prevent holes.

FRONT: With size 4 needles, cast on 96 sts. Work in K1, P1, ribbing for 3 inches. Change to size 6 needles and increase 12 sts evenly spaced on next row working in st st. Continue in st st and work charted design, binding off and decreasing as indicated. Place 24 sts in center of front on holder to be picked up later for neck ribbing.

BACK: Work to match front. Place 35 sts in center of back on holder for neck ribbing.

SLEEVES: With size 4 needles, cast on 42 sts. Work in K1, P1, ribbing for 3 inches. Change to size 6 needles and increase 6 sts evenly spaced in next row using st st. Work sleeves according to charted design.

Sew shoulder seams.

NECK: With size 4 needles and right side facing, pick up and K across 35 sts on back holder, pick up and K 15 sts to front holder, K across 24 sts on front holder, and pick up and K 16 sts to back. Total 90 sts. K1, P1, in ribbing for 1 inch. Bind off loosely in ribbing.

Sew sleeves in place. Sew underarm and sleeve seams. Weave in loose threads.

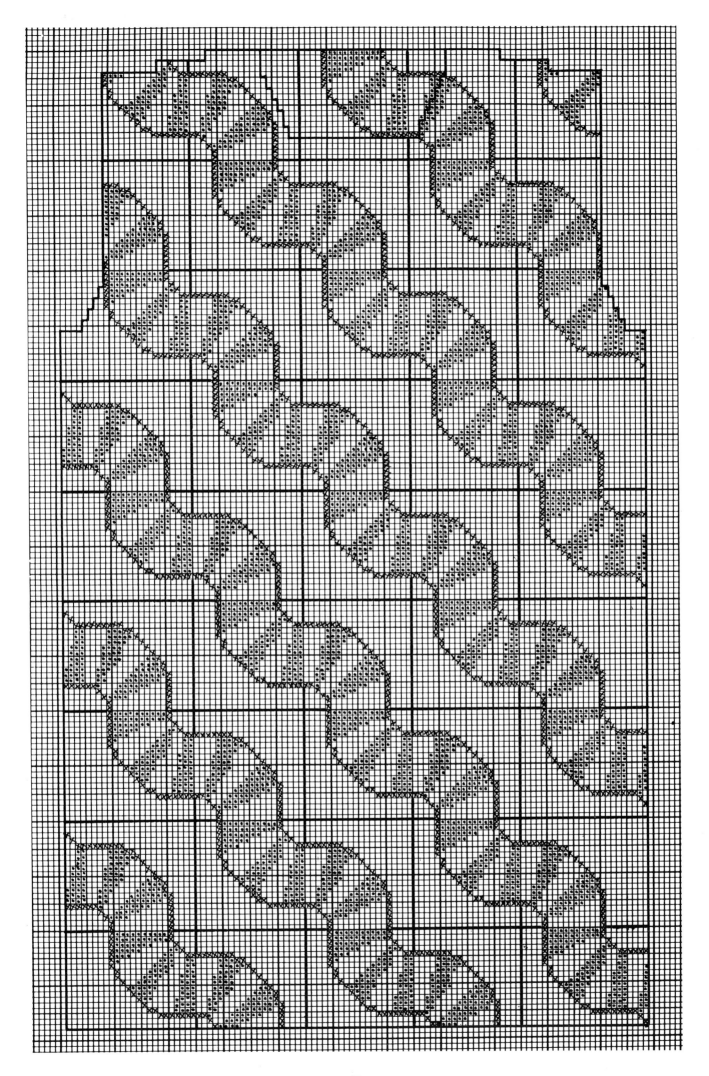

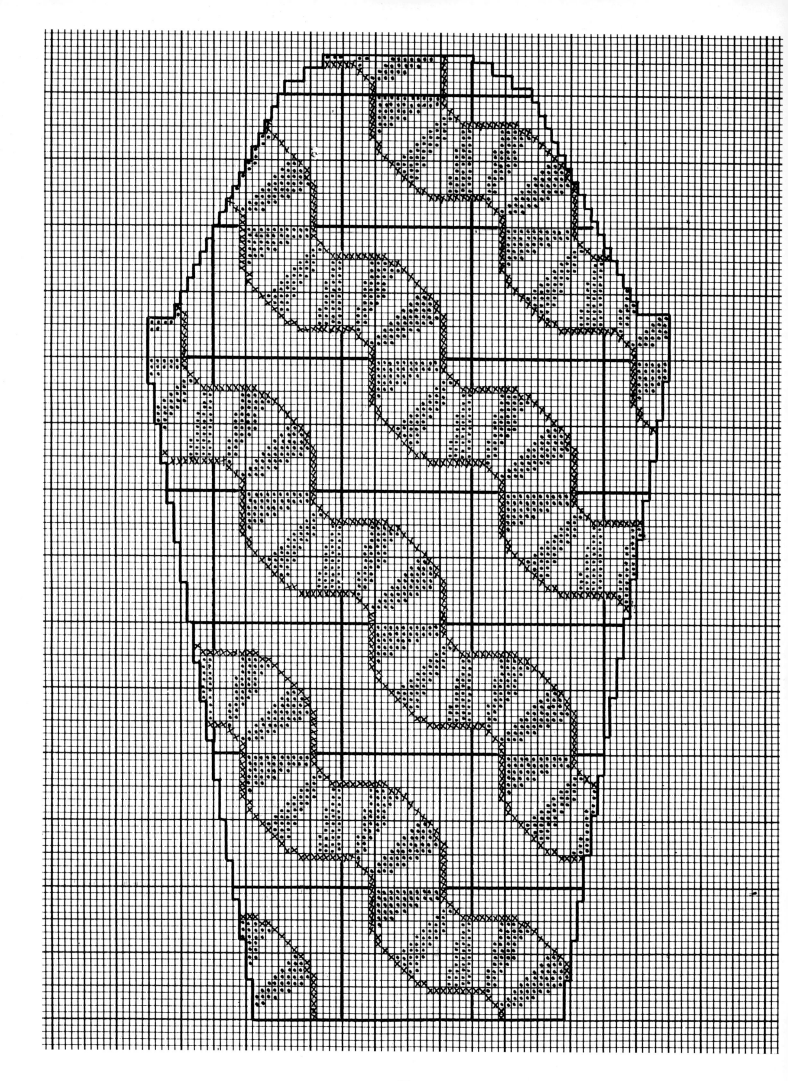

Patchwork Star
Crew-Neck Pullover

PATCHWORK STAR CREW-NECK PULLOVER

A bright and cheerful adaptation of a classic 19th-century quilt, this charming sweater works up well in any color combination. The textured look in the white squares is created by working diagonal lines in garter stitch.

MATERIALS: 14 oz. white in knitting worsted or yarn to give the recommended gauge below. 12 oz. blue, 4 oz. red, 4 oz. yellow. Yarn should *NOT* be carried across the back of work.

NEEDLES: Size 4 and 7. One set of double-point needles size 4.

GAUGE: 4½ sts = 1 inch. 6½ rows = 1 inch. Correct needle size if necessary.

SIZE: These directions are for a size 44″ finished garment. Measurements are: length to underarm 16½″, length to shoulder 24½″, length of sleeve to underarm 18″.

To alter size, see instructions for SIZING.

NOTE: Do *NOT* carry yarn across. Use a separate yarn for each color change and twist old and new yarn around each other to prevent holes. Loose ends are woven in later.

FRONT: With size 4 needles and main color, cast on 80 sts. Work in K1, P1, ribbing for 3 inches. Change to size 7 needles and increase 20 sts in next row working in st st. Continue in st st and work charted design, binding off and decreasing as indicated. Place center 16 sts on holder for neck ribbing.

BACK: Work to match front. Fill in pattern at neck to shoulders and place 36 sts in center of back on holder for neck ribbing.

SLEEVES: With size 4 needles, cast on 34 sts. Work in K1, P1, ribbing for 3 inches. Change to size 7 needles and increase 10 sts on next row, evenly spaced working in st st. Work sleeves according to charted design, measuring length as work is done to correct length.

Sew shoulder seams.

NECK: With size 4 double-point needles and right side facing, pick up and K across 36 sts on back holder, pick up and K 14 sts to front holder, K across 16 sts on front holder, and pick up and K 14 sts to back. Total 80 sts. K1, P1, in ribbing for 1 inch. Bind off loosely in ribbing.

Sew sleeves in place, as marked on pattern. Sew underarm and sleeve seams. Weave in loose threads.

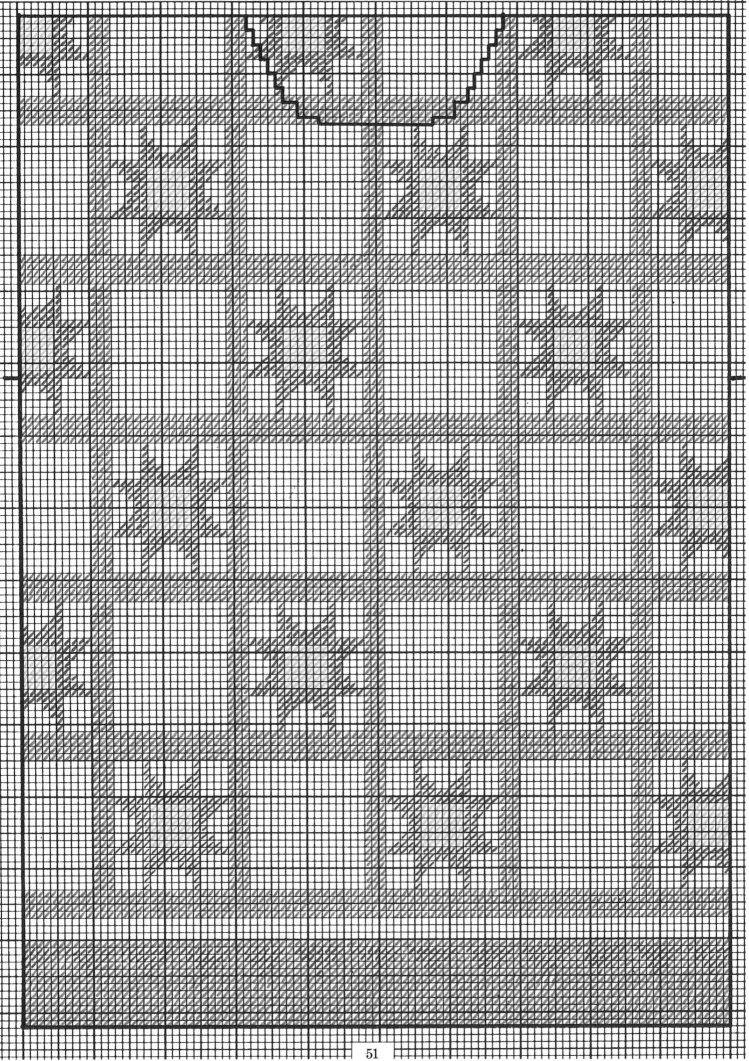

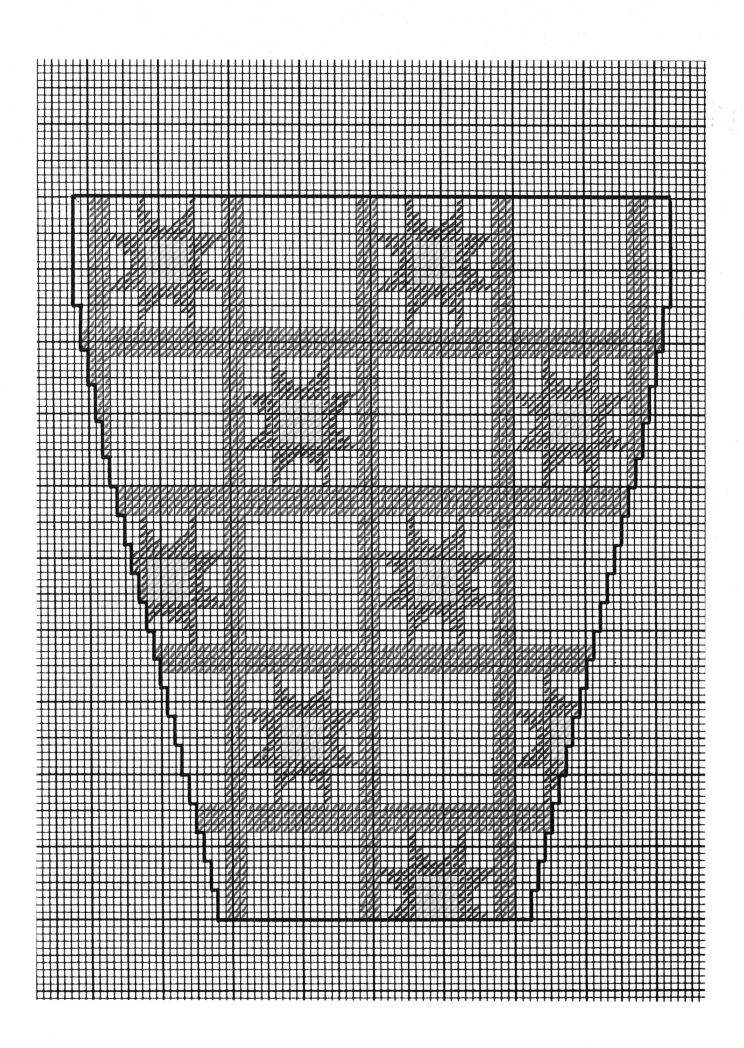

Reindeer
Crew-Neck Pullover

REINDEER CREW-NECK PULLOVER

This is no ordinary "classic" reindeer sweater. This one comes from a wonderful 19th-century hooked rug. Folky and fun, knit it in a wild array of colors, or a contrasting light and dark. Whichever you choose, your reindeer will draw lots of comments.

MATERIALS: 14-16 oz. each of two contrasting colors in sport-weight wool, cotton, or yarn to give recommended gauge below. 2 oz. green for trees. If making multi-colored sweater, divide total ounces of two main colors by number of colors using.

NEEDLES: Size 4 and 6. One set of double-point needles size 4.

GAUGE: 5½ sts = 1 inch. 6½ rows = 1 inch. Correct needle size if necessary.

SIZE: These directions are for a size 39" finished garment using inside lines. Measurements are: length to underarm 18", length to shoulder 25", length of sleeve to underarm 19".

For size 42" use outside lines and larger neck opening. Enlarge sleeve by 3 sts on each side.

To alter size, see instructions for SIZING. An oversize sweater can be made using this pattern with worsted weight wool and size 5 and 7 needles.

NOTE: Do *NOT* carry yarn across. Use a new yarn for each color change and twist old and new yarns around each other to prevent holes.

FRONT: With size 4 needles, cast on 96 sts. Work in K1, P1, ribbing for 3 inches. Change to size 6 needles and increase 12 sts evenly spaced on next row working in st st. Continue in st st and work charted design, using colors of choice, binding off and decreasing as indicated. Place the 24 sts in center of front on holder to be picked up later for neck ribbing.

BACK: Work to match front. Fill in pattern at neck to shoulders and place 35 sts in center of back on holder for neck ribbing.

SLEEVES: With size 4 needles, cast on 42 sts. Work in K1, P1, ribbing for 3 inches. Change to size 6 needles and increase 6 sts evenly spaced in next row using st st. Work sleeves according to charted design.

Sew shoulder seams.

NECK: With size 4 double-point needles and right side facing, pick up and K across 35 sts on back holder, pick up and K 15 sts to front holder, K across 24 sts on front holder, and pick up and K 16 sts to back. Total 90 sts. K1, P1, in ribbing for 1 inch. Bind off loosely in ribbing.

Sew sleeves in place. Sew underarm and sleeve seams. Weave in loose threads.

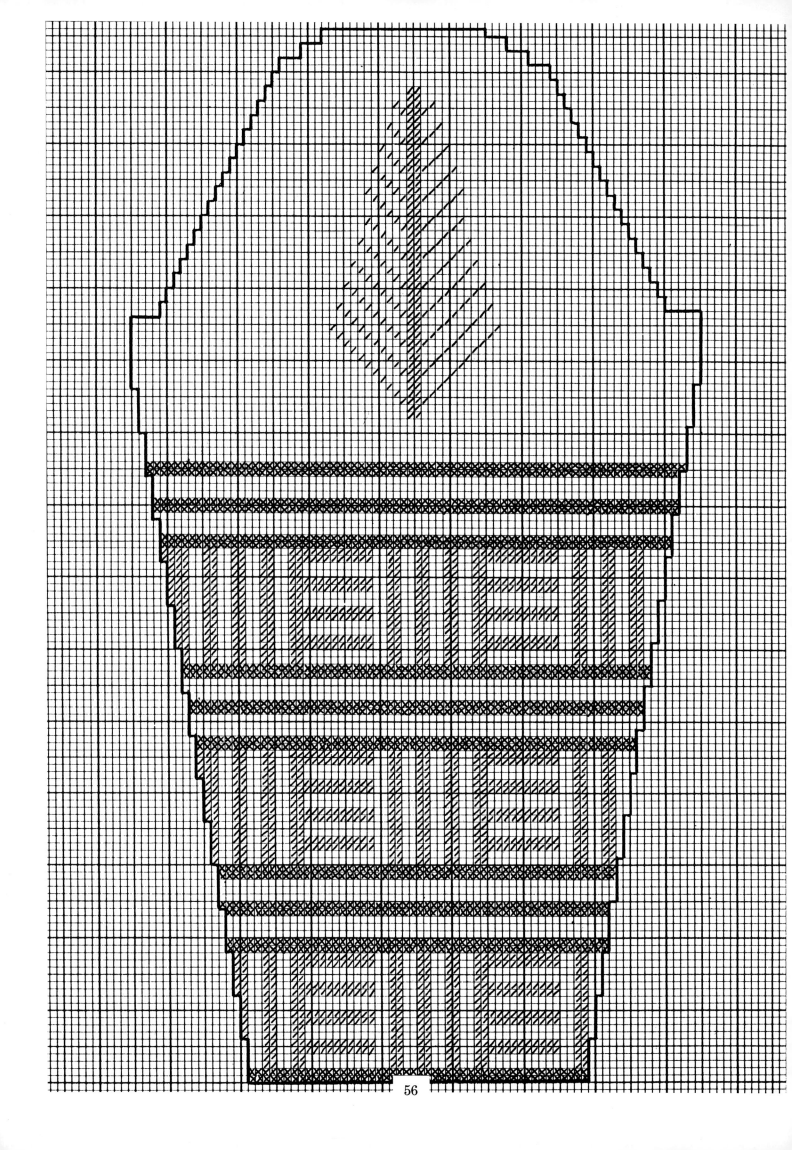

Flower and Vine
Crew-Neck Pullover

FLOWER AND VINE CREW-NECK PULLOVER

This striking flower and vine grid design is great in any color scheme: russets, golds, and browns for fall, and pastels for spring. Metallic yarns can dress it up for evening or holiday flair.

MATERIALS: 16 to 18 oz. of background color in knitting worsted weight yarn. 4 oz. dark green for leaves and vines, 4 oz. each of 2 different colors for petals, ½ oz. of two different colors for center of flowers.

NEEDLES: Size 4 and 7. One set of double-point needles size 4.

GAUGE: 4½ sts = 1 inch. 6½ rows = 1 inch. Correct needle size if necessary.

SIZE: These directions are for a size 44″ finished garment. Measurements are: length to underarm 16½″, length to shoulder 24½″, length of sleeve to underarm 18″.

To alter size, see instructions for SIZING.

NOTE: Do *NOT* carry yarn across. Use a separate yarn for each color change and twist old and new yarn around each other to prevent holes. Loose ends are woven in later.

FRONT: With size 4 needles and main color, cast on 80 sts. Work in K1, P1, ribbing for 3 inches. Change to size 7 needles and increase 20 sts in next row working in st st. Continue in st st and work charted design, binding off and decreasing as indicated. Place center 16 sts on holder for neck ribbing.

BACK: Work to match front. Place 36 sts in center of back on holder for neck ribbing.

SLEEVES: With size 4 needles, cast on 34 sts. Work in K1, P1, ribbing for 3 inches. Change to size 7 needles and increase 10 sts on next row evenly spaced working in st st. Work sleeves according to charted design, measuring length as work is done to correct length.

Sew shoulder seams.

NECK: With size 4 double-point needles and right side facing, pick up and K across 36 sts on back holder, pick up and K 14 sts to front holder, K across 16 sts on front holder, and pick up and K 14 sts to back. Total 80 sts. K1, P1, in ribbing for 1 inch. Bind off loosely in ribbing.

Sew sleeves in place, as marked on pattern. Sew underarm and sleeve seams. Weave in loose threads.

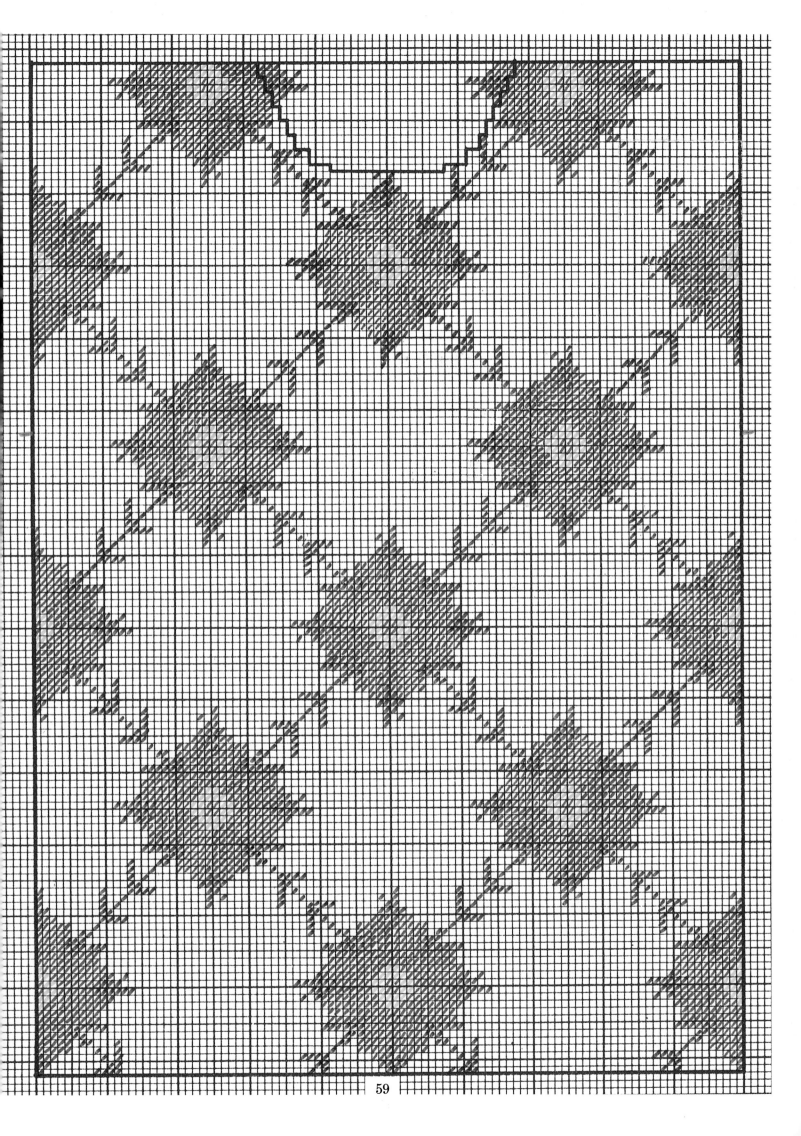

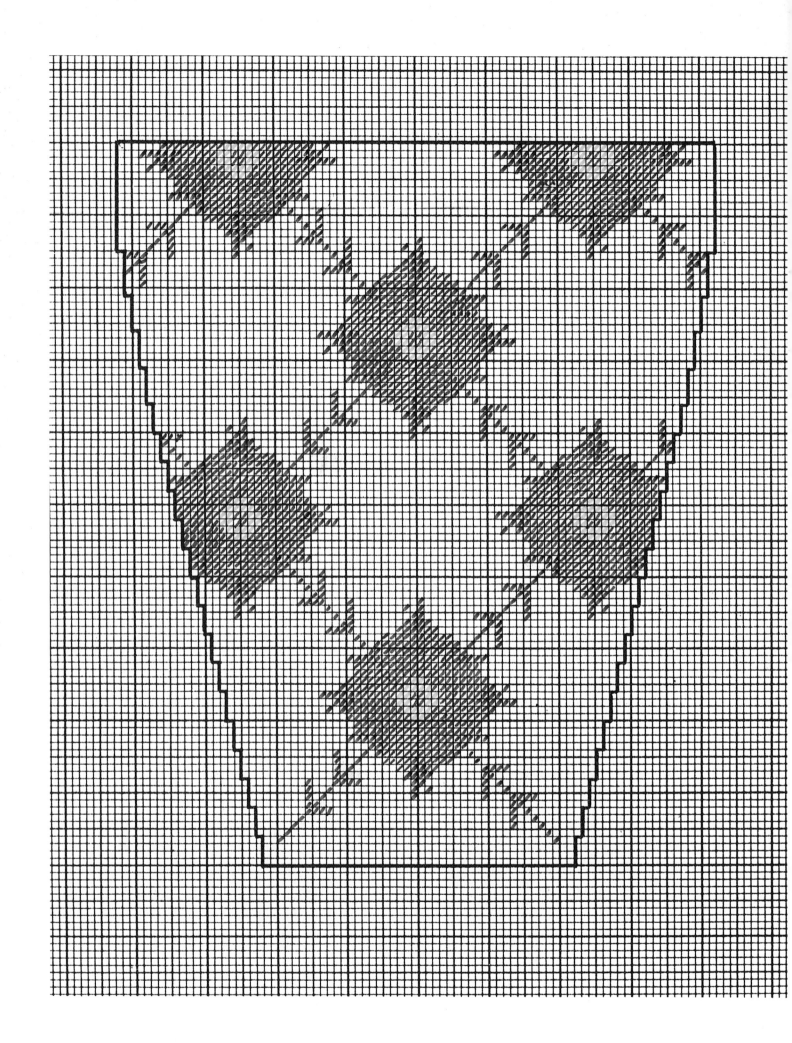

Flamingo and Palm Tree
Collared Pullover

FLAMINGO AND PALM TREE COLLARED PULLOVER

An Art Deco rendition of Country, this is a popular motif for summer or resort. It's "in," lots of fun, and quick to knit.

MATERIALS: 14 to 16 oz. cotton or wool in weight to give recommended gauge below, in background color. 2 to 3 oz. each of brown, sand, blue, bright green, light brown, and hot pink.

NEEDLES: Size 3 and 5. Size 3 circular needle.

GAUGE: 6 sts = 1 inch. 7-7½ rows = 1 inch. Check yarn band as cottons are very irregular. Calculate finished length and add or delete rows if necessary.

SIZE: These directions are for a size 40″ finished sweater.

To alter size, see instructions for SIZING.

FRONT: With smaller needles and main color, cast on 104 sts. Work in K2, P2, ribbing for 1½ inches increasing 16 sts across last row. Change to larger needles and follow graph, increasing, decreasing, and binding off as indicated.

BACK: Work as for front, omitting tree and flamingo and continuing stripes across bottom matching sides. Increase, decrease, and bind off as shown. Place center sts on holder for neck.

SLEEVES: With smaller needles, cast on 40 sts in main color. Work in K2, P2, ribbing for 1½ inches, increasing 10 sts evenly spaced across last row. Work in st st following charted design, increasing, decreasing, and binding off as indicated.

Sew shoulder seams.

COLLAR: With right side facing, and circular needle, begin at center front, pick up and K 21 sts along right front neck to shoulder, 34 sts along back neck, and 21 sts along left neck to center front — 76 sts. Join and place marker for beginning of round. NEXT ROUND: K1, *P2, K2; rep for *, end K1. Repeat last round 3 times more. Continue working back and forth in rib as follows:
NEXT ROW: right side — decrease 1 st, rib to last st, decrease 1 st. Continue in K2, P2, until collar measures 3 inches. Bind off in ribbing.

Place markers 8½ inches down from shoulders on front and back for armholes. Sew top of sleeves between markers. Sew side and sleeve seams. Weave in threads.

KEY: ✘ BLUE, ▮ GREEN, ✚ PALE PINK,
⁄ PINK, • BROWN, – TAN

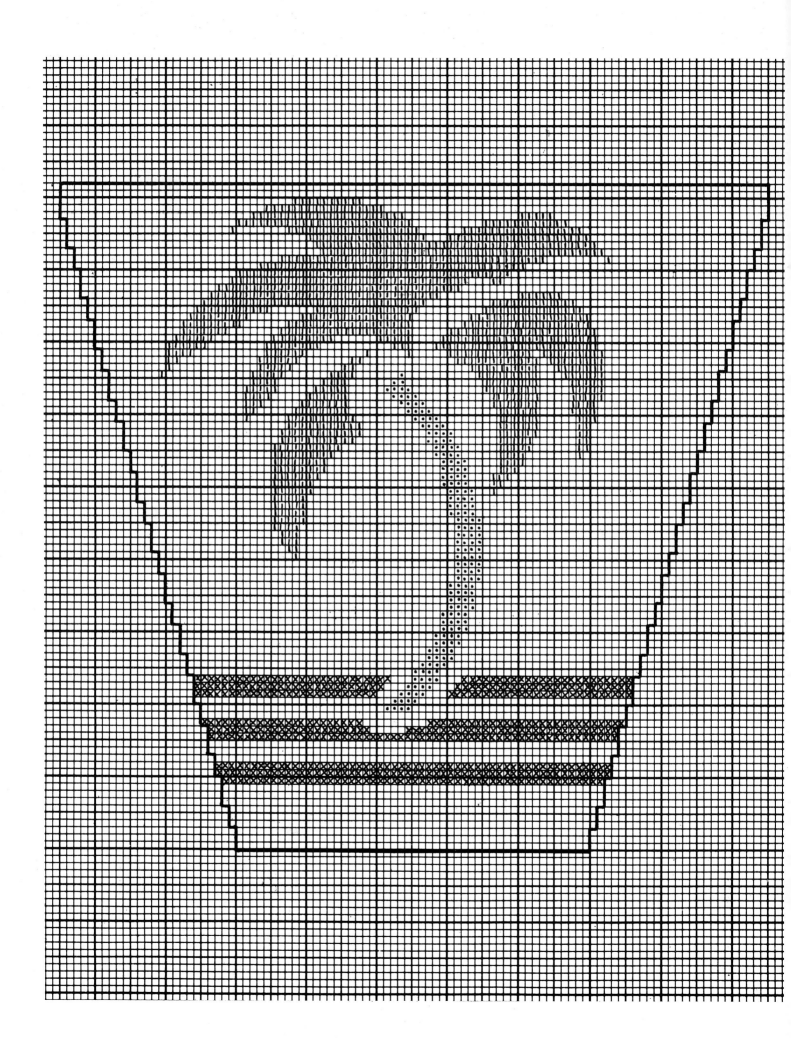

64

Moored Boats
Crew-Neck Pullover

MOORED BOATS CREW-NECK PULLOVER

The "yachty" look of this sweater will make it a hit with all your sailors. Knit in two colors, the boats are silhouetted against the background. For lots of bright color, work the boats in different shades and make the sleeves multi-color stripes.

MATERIALS: 18 to 20 oz. of background color in knitting worsted weight or other yarn to give the recommended gauge below. 6 to 8 oz. of contrasting color or combination of colors for boats and stripes.

NEEDLES: Size 4 and 7. One set of double-point needles, size 4.

GAUGE: 4½ sts = 1 inch, 6½-7 rows = 1 inch.

SIZE: These directions are for a size 42"-44" oversize sweater.

To alter size see instructions for SIZING.

NOTE: This is a drop shoulder and does not hit at the usual shoulder seam. Check sleeves for length while knitting.

FRONT: With main color and size 4 needles, cast on 84 sts and work in K1, P1, ribbing for 2 inches. Increase 16 sts evenly spaced across next row of ribbing. Change to larger needles and working in st st follow graphed design. Increase, decrease, and bind off as indicated. Place center sts of neck on holder for neck ribbing.

BACK: Work as for front, placing center 36 sts on holder for neck ribbing.

SLEEVES: With smaller needles and main color cast on 34 sts. Work in K1, P1, ribbing for 2 inches. Increase 10 sts in next row of ribbing, 44 sts. Change to larger needles and work in st st following charted design. Increase and bind off as indicated.

Sew shoulder seams.

NECK: With right sides facing and double-point needles, begin at right shoulder, pick up and K 36 sts along back neck, 44 sts along front neck — 80 sts. Work in K1, P1, ribbing for 1 inch. Bind off loosely in ribbing.

Sew sleeves to front and back. Sew sleeve and side seams.

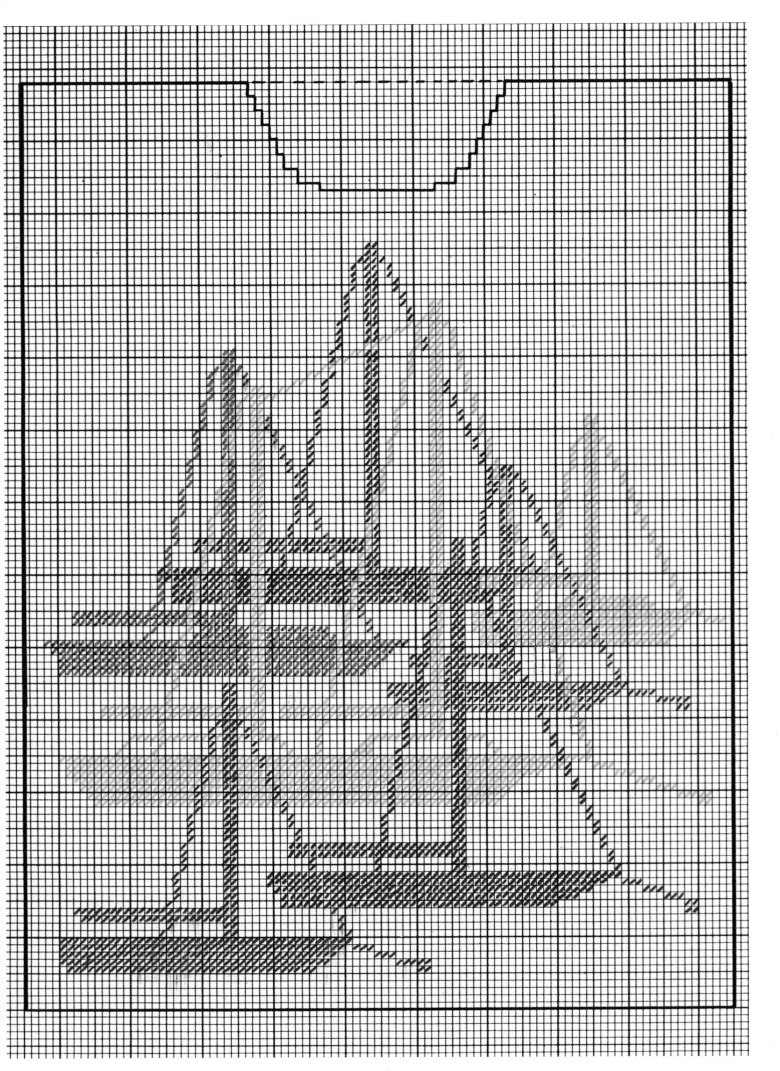

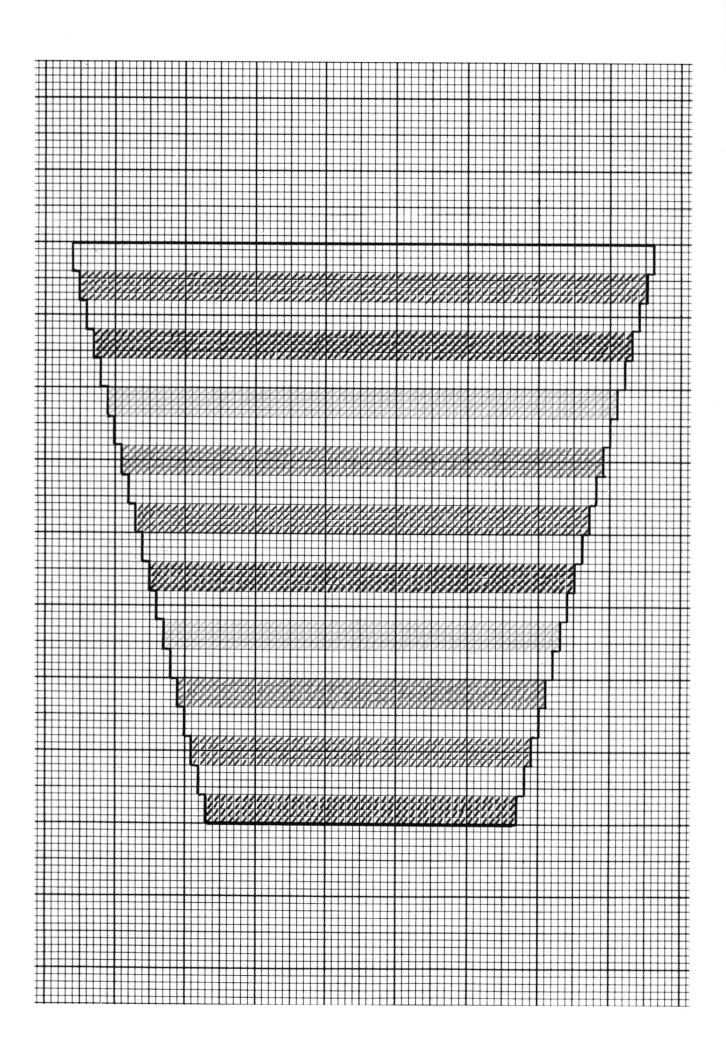

Checked Flower
Crew-Neck Pullover

CHECKED FLOWER CREW-NECK PULLOVER

A wonderful sweater for dress or casual, this geometric design is easy to knit and striking to wear. Flowers can be knit in different colors for a very visual effect.

MATERIALS: 14-16 oz. each of two contrasting colors of sport-weight wool, cotton, or yarn to give recommended gauge below. 2-3 oz. of color for center of flowers.

NEEDLES: Size 4 and 6. One set of double-point needles size 4.

GAUGE: 5½ sts = 1 inch. 6½ rows = 1 inch. Correct needle size if necessary.

SIZE: These directions are for a size 39″ finished garment using inside lines. Measurements are: length to underarm 18″, length to shoulder 26″, length of sleeve to underarm 19″.

For size 42″ use outside lines and larger neck opening. Enlarge sleeve by 3 sts on each side.

To alter size, see instructions for SIZING. An oversize sweater can be made using this pattern with worsted weight wool and size 5 and 7 needles.

NOTE: Do *NOT* carry yarn across. Use a new yarn for each color change and twist old and new yarns around each other to prevent holes.

FRONT: With size 4 needles, cast on 96 sts. Work in K1, P1, ribbing for 3 inches. Change to size 6 needles and increase 12 sts evenly spaced on next row working in st st. Continue in st st and work charted design, using colors of choice in various blocks, binding off and decreasing as indicated. Place the 24 sts in center of front on holder to be picked up later for neck ribbing.

BACK: Work to match front. Fill in pattern at neck to shoulders and place 35 sts in center of back on holder for neck ribbing.

SLEEVES: With size 4 needles, cast on 42 sts. Work in K1, P1, ribbing for 3 inches. Change to size 6 needles and increase 6 sts evenly spaced in next row using st st. Work sleeves according to charted design.

Sew shoulder seams.

NECK: With size 4 double-point needles and right side facing, pick up and K across 35 sts on back holder, pick up and K 15 sts to front holder, K across 24 sts on front holder, and pick up and K 16 sts to back. Total 90 sts. K1, P1, in ribbing for 1 inch. Bind off loosely in ribbing.

Sew sleeves in place. Sew underarm and sleeve seams. Weave in loose threads.

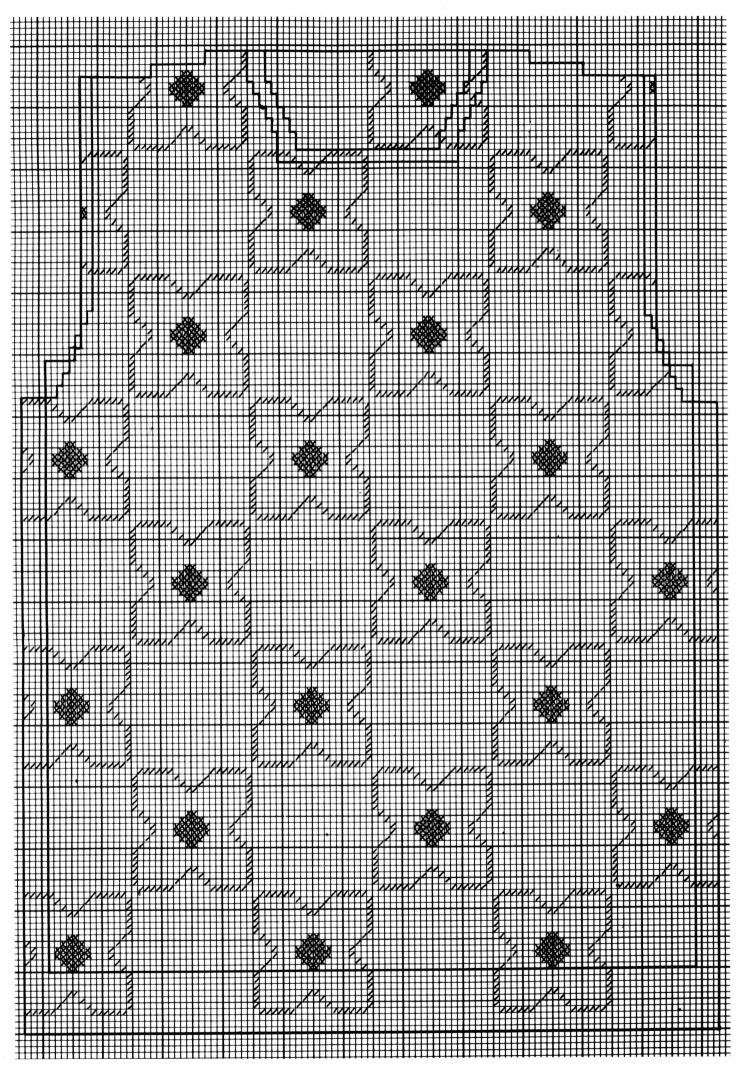

71

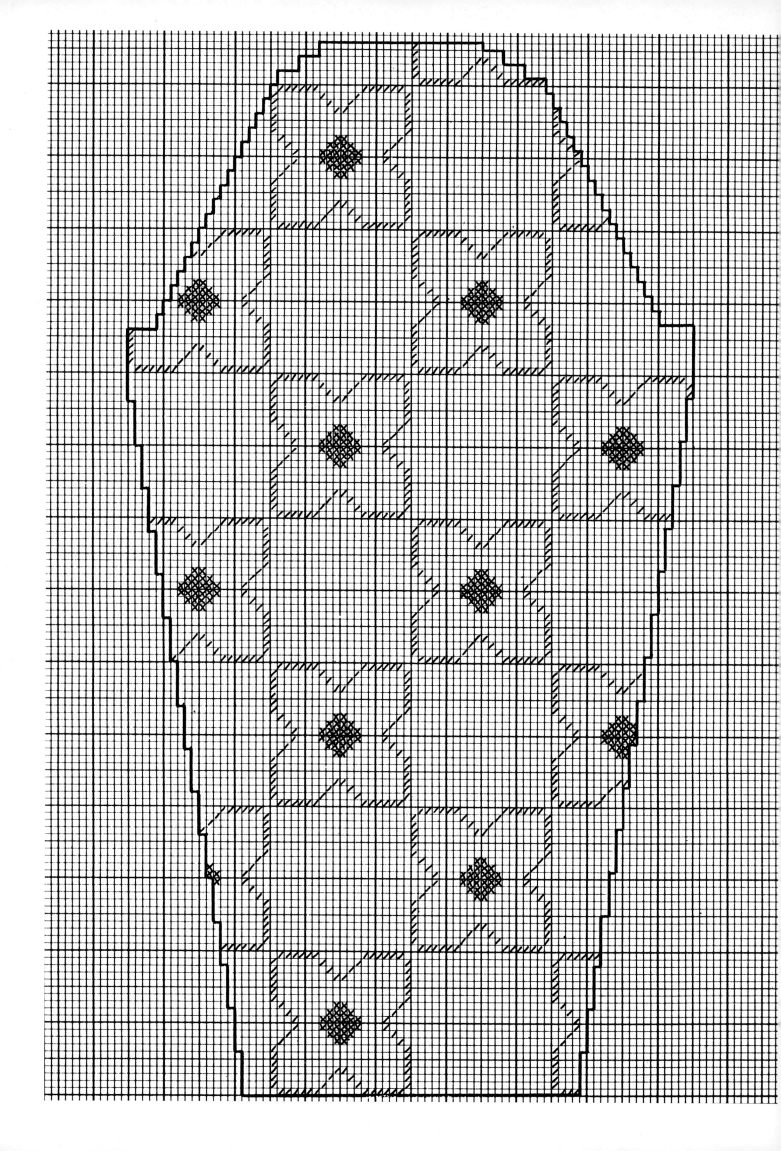

Oriental Rug
Crew-Neck Pullover

ORIENTAL RUG CREW-NECK PULLOVER

From the intricate patterns in an Oriental rug we have chosen a few motifs to combine in a sweater. And what a striking design it turned out to be! Great for men or women, the colors are rich and bold, and the knitting easy.

MATERIALS: 20-22 oz. main color in knitting worsted or yarn to give the recommended gauge below. 4-6 oz. dark blue, 4-6 oz. burgundy, 4-6 oz. tan. Yarn should *NOT* be carried across the back of work.

NEEDLES: Size 4 and 7. One set of double-point needles size 4.

GAUGE: 4½ sts = 1 inch. 6½ rows = 1 inch. Correct needle size if necessary.

SIZE: These directions are for a size 44″ finished garment. Measurements are: length to underarm 16½″, length to shoulder 24½″, length of sleeve to underarm 18″.

To alter size, see instructions for SIZING.

NOTE: Do *NOT* carry yarn across. Use a separate yarn for each color change and twist old and new yarn around each other to prevent holes. Loose ends are woven in later.

FRONT: With size 4 needles and main color, cast on 80 sts. Work in K1, P1, ribbing for 3 inches. Change to size 7 needles and increase 20 sts in next row working in st st. Continue in st st and work charted design, binding off and decreasing as indicated. Place center 16 sts on holder for neck ribbing.

BACK: Work to match front. Place 36 sts in center of back on holder for neck ribbing.

SLEEVES: With size 4 needles, cast on 34 sts. Work in K1, P1, ribbing for 3 inches. Change to size 7 needles and increase 10 sts on next row evenly spaced working in st st. Work sleeves according to charted design, measuring length as work is done to correct length.

Sew shoulder seams.

NECK: With size 4 double-point needles and right side facing, pick up and K across 36 sts on back holder, pick up and K 14 sts to front holder, K across 16 sts on front holder, and pick up and K 14 sts to back. Total 80 sts. K1, P1, in ribbing for 1 inch. Bind off loosely in ribbing.

Sew sleeves in place, as marked on pattern. Sew underarm and sleeve seams. Weave in loose threads.

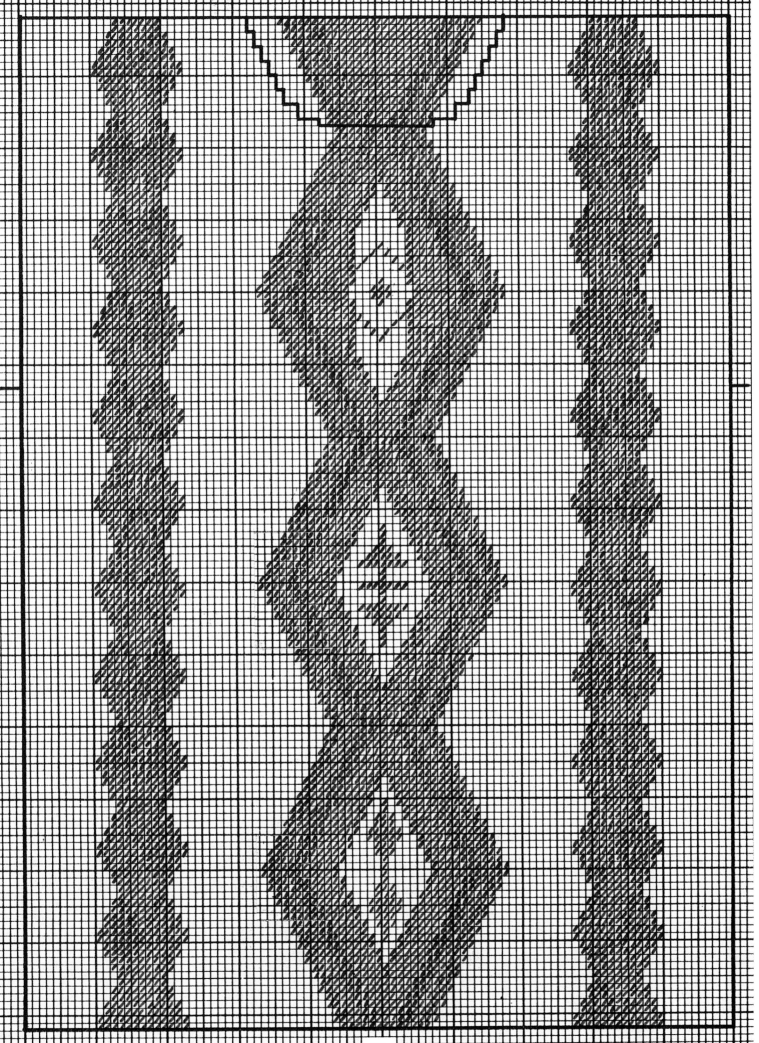

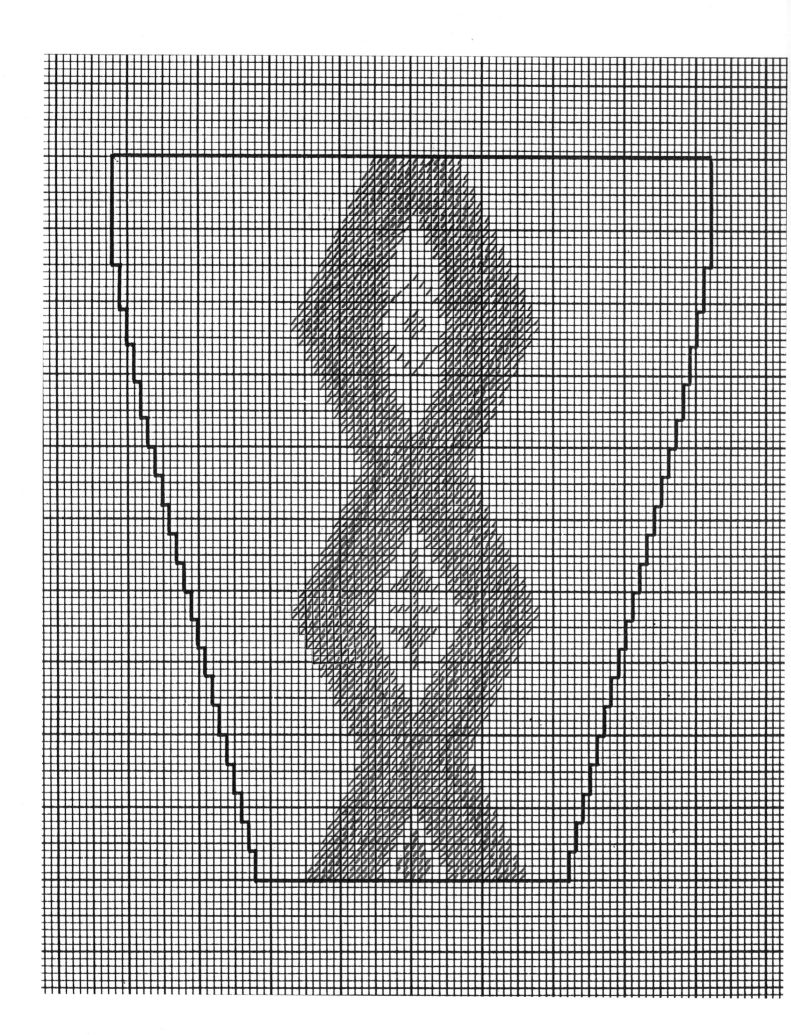

Christmas Goose
Crew-Neck Pullover

CHRISTMAS GOOSE CREW-NECK PULLOVER

A special country seasonal sweater, the traditional goose is decked out for the holidays with a big bow. Stripes give a candy cane look to the background and make for a festive Christmas sweater. It also looks great with a white background and green stripe.

MATERIALS: 12 to 15 oz. main color in knitting worsted or yarn to give the recommended gauge below. 4 to 6 oz. of stripe color, 1 oz. of color for checkerboard frame, 1 oz. of color for goose, 1 oz. of background color inside frame. Small amount of color for ribbon, beak, feet, and eye.

NEEDLES: Size 4 and 7. One set of double-point needles, size 4.

GAUGE: 4½ sts = 1 inch, 6½ rows = 1 inch.

SIZE: These directions are for a size 44″ oversize sweater.

To alter size see instructions for SIZING.

NOTE—This is a drop shoulder and does not hit at the usual shoulder seam. Check sleeves for length while knitting.

FRONT: With main color and size 4 needles, cast on 84 sts and work in K1, P1, ribbing for 2 inches. Increase 16 sts evenly spaced across next row of ribbing. Change to larger needles and working in st st follow graphed design. Increase, decrease, and bind off as indicated. Place center sts of neck on holder for neck ribbing.

BACK: Work as for front, omitting central motif, but continuing stripes.

SLEEVES: With smaller needles and main color cast on 34 sts. Work in K1, P1, ribbing for 2 inches. Increase 10 sts in next row of ribbing, 44 sts. Change to larger needles and work in st st following charted design. Increase and bind off as indicated.

Sew shoulder seams.

NECK: With right sides facing and double-point needles, begin at right shoulder, pick up and K 36 sts along back neck, 44 sts along front neck—80 sts. Work in K1, P1, ribbing for 1 inch. Bind off loosely in ribbing.

Sew sleeves to front and back. Sew sleeve and side seams.

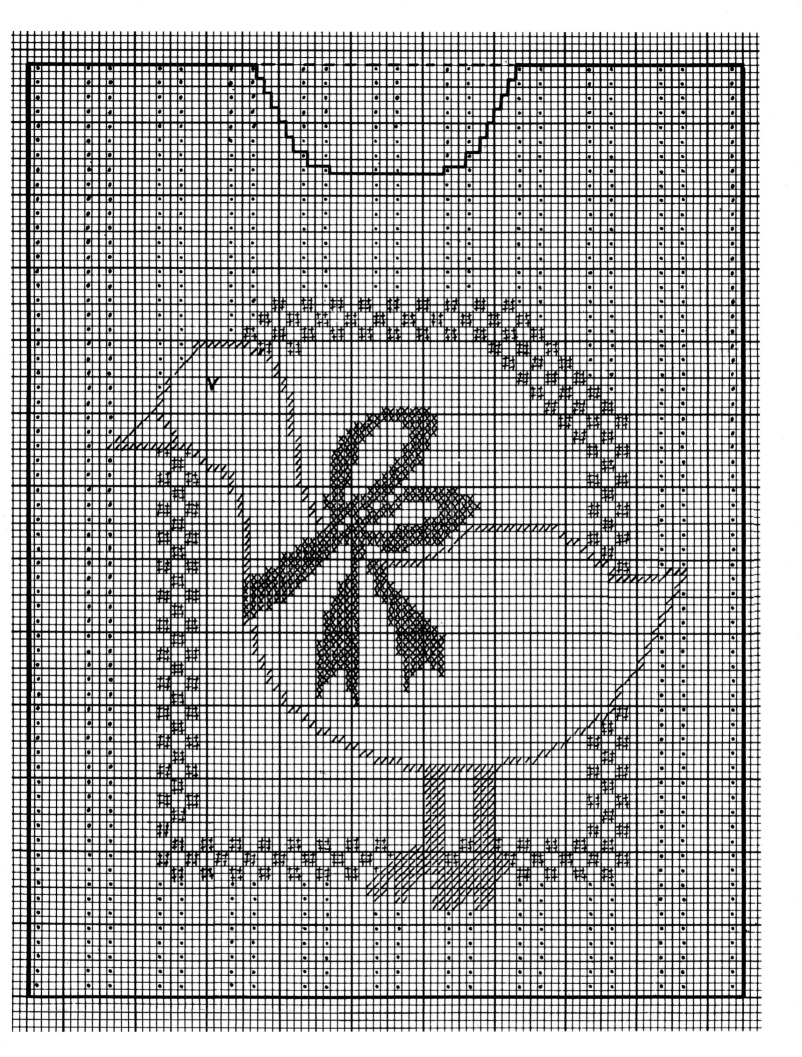

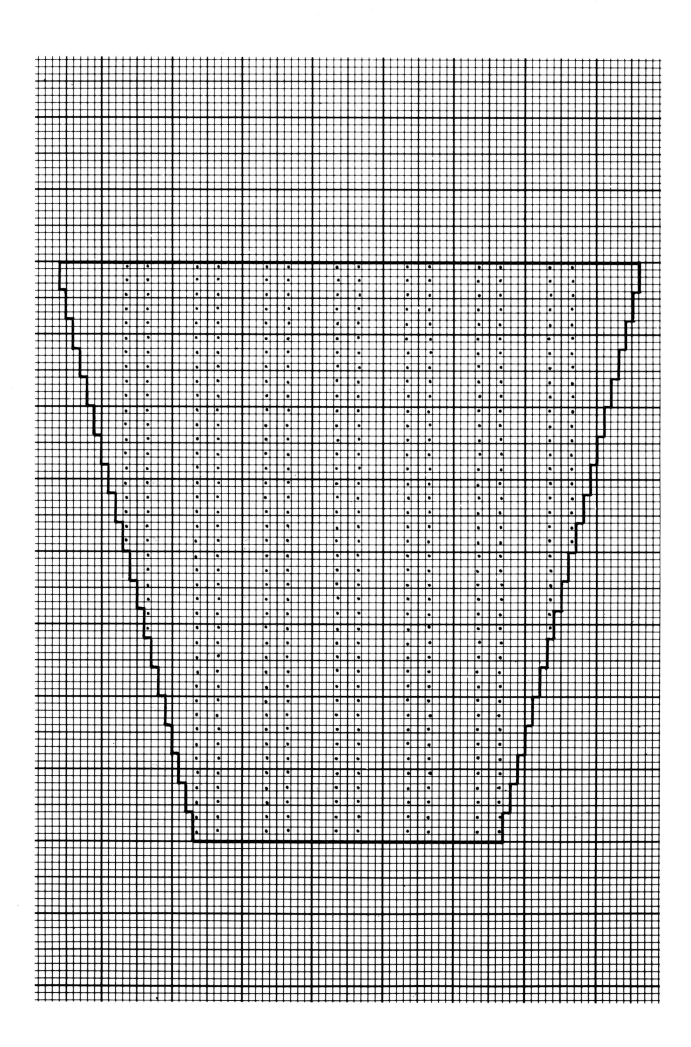

Nine Patch
Crew-Neck Pullover

NINE PATCH CREW-NECK PULLOVER

In the bygone days of quiltmaking, little girls were given small squares of cloth to assemble. They would make three rows of three squares and then sew them together to make a Nine Patch design. The completed squares would later be sewn together to make small quilts. Our Nine Patch sweater is knit all at one time and can have dramatic effects depending on the colors used.

MATERIALS: 8-10 oz. of four different colors in knitting sport weight or yarn to give recommended gauge below. 4 oz. white or contrast color. Yarn should *NOT* be carried across back.

NEEDLES: Size 4 and 6. One set of double-point needles size 4.

GAUGE: 5½ sts = 1 inch. 6½ rows = 1 inch. Correct needle size if necessary.

SIZE: These directions are for a size 38″ finished garment. Measurements are: length to underarm 18″, length to shoulder 25″, length of sleeve to underarm 19″.

To alter size, see instructions for SIZING. An oversize sweater can be made using this pattern with worsted weight wool and size 5 and 7 needles.

NOTE: Do *NOT* carry yarn across. Use a new yarn for each color change and twist old and new yarns around each other to prevent holes.

FRONT: With size 4 needles, cast on 100 sts. Work in K1, P1, ribbing for 3 inches. Change to size 6 needles and increase 16 sts evenly spaced on next row working in st st. Continue in st st and work charted design, using colors of choice in various blocks, binding off and decreasing as indicated. Place the 26 sts in center of front on holder to be picked up later for neck ribbing.

BACK: Work to match front. Fill in pattern at neck to shoulders and place 36 sts in center of back on holder for neck ribbing.

SLEEVES: With size 4 needles, cast on 42 sts. Work in K1, P1, ribbing for 3 inches. Change to size 6 needles and increase 6 sts evenly spaced in next row using st st. Work sleeves according to charted design.

Sew shoulder seams.

NECK: With size 4 double-point needles and right side facing, pick up and K across 36 sts on back holder, pick up and K 15 sts to front holder, K across 26 sts on front holder, and pick up and K 16 sts to back. Total 93 sts. K1, P1, in ribbing for 1 inch. Bind off loosely in ribbing.

Sew sleeves in place. Sew underarm and sleeve seams. Weave in loose threads.

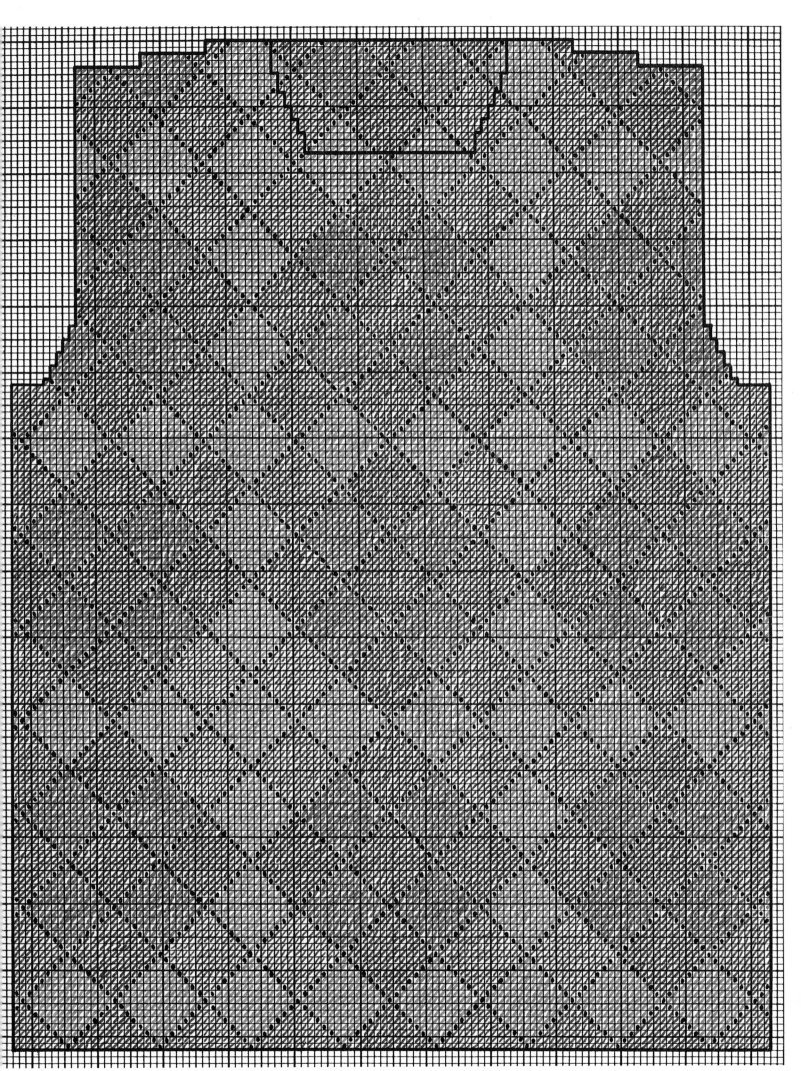

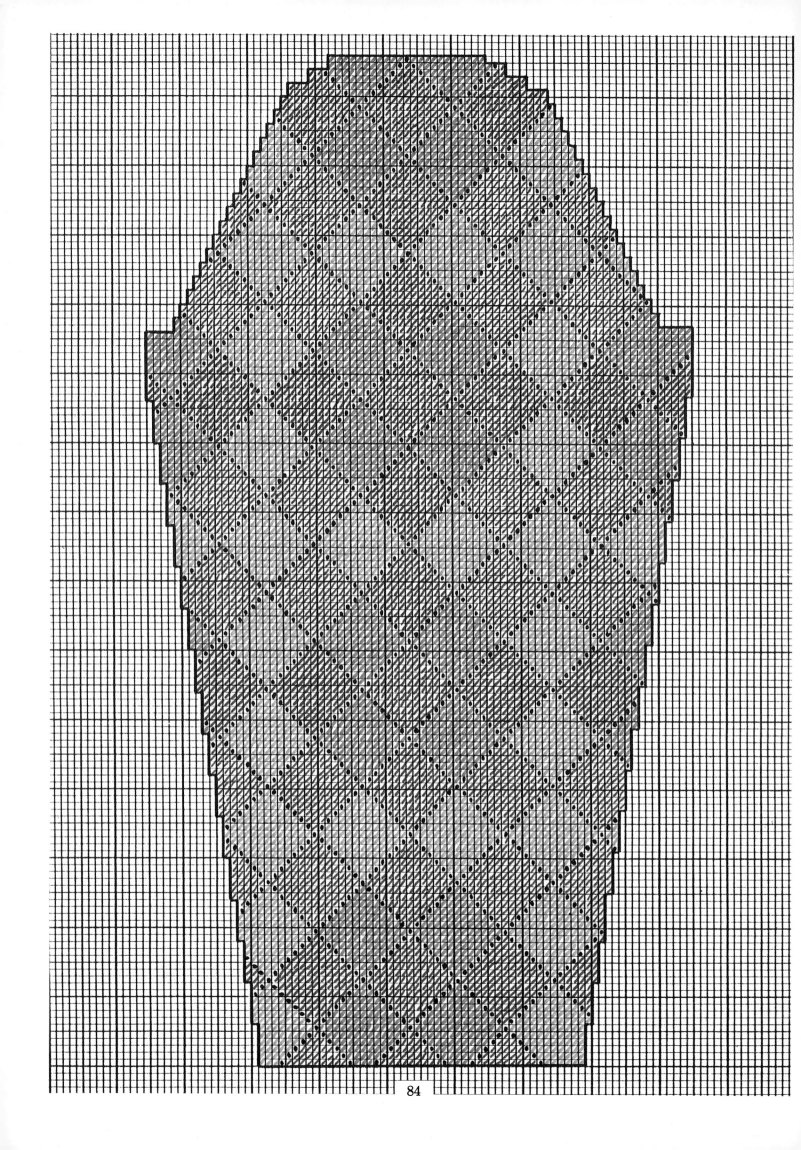

"Out-of-Africa" Cardigan

"OUT-OF-AFRICA" CARDIGAN

A stunning "safari" look is captured by this jungle design. The back and sleeves continue the bottom border of tall grasses and wildflowers. We recommend knitting the animals in and using duplicate stitch on the flowers.

MATERIALS:	18-22 oz. dark green background in sport-weight wool, cotton, or yarn to give recommended gauge below. 4 oz. light green, 1 oz. each of black, yellow, tan, light brown, dark brown, grey. Small amounts of colors for flowers.
NEEDLES:	Size 4 and 5.
GAUGE:	5½ sts = 1 inch. 7 rows = 1 inch. Correct needle size if necessary.
SIZE:	These directions are for a size 42″ finished garment. Measurements are: length to underarm 17½″, length to shoulder 27″, length of sleeve to underarm 20″.
NOTE:	Do *NOT* carry yarn across. Use a new yarn for each color change and twist old and new yarns around each other to prevent holes.
LEFT FRONT:	With smaller needles cast on 52 sts. Work in K1, P1, ribbing for 2 inches. Change to larger needles and increase 6 sts evenly spaced over the next row while working in st st (58 sts). Continue in st st and work charted design, binding off and decreasing as indicated. Place 12 sts at neck edge on holder for neck ribbing.
RIGHT FRONT:	Work as for left front, using chart for right side.
BACK:	With smaller needles cast on 108 sts. Work in K1, P1, ribbing for 2 inches. Change to larger needles and increase 15 sts evenly spaced over the next row working in st st (123 sts). Continue in st st and work charted design. Bind off, placing center 44 sts on holder.
SLEEVES:	With smaller needles cast on 47 sts. Work in K1, P1, ribbing for 3 inches. Change to larger needles and increase 9 sts evenly spaced across next row in st st (56 sts). Continue in st st and work charted design, increasing as indicated. Knit to desired length, bind off.

Sew shoulder seams.

NECK:	With smaller needles and right side facing, pick up 12 sts from holder, 20 sts to back, 44 sts from back holder, 20 sts to left front, and 12 sts from holder. 108 sts. Work in K1, P1, ribbing for 1¼ inches. Bind off loosely in ribbing.
LEFT FRONT BAND:	With smaller needles cast on 9 sts. Work in K1, P1, ribbing to fit length of sweater. Bind off loosely in ribbing. Attach to left front in flat running stitch.
RIGHT FRONT BAND:	With smaller needles cast on 9 sts. Work in K1, P1, ribbing making 7 buttonholes, the first and last 1 inch from edge, the others evenly spaced. Buttonholes: Bind off 4 sts, next row cast on 4 sts. Attach to right front in flat running stitch.

Sew sleeves in place. Sew underarm and sleeve seams. Weave in loose threads.

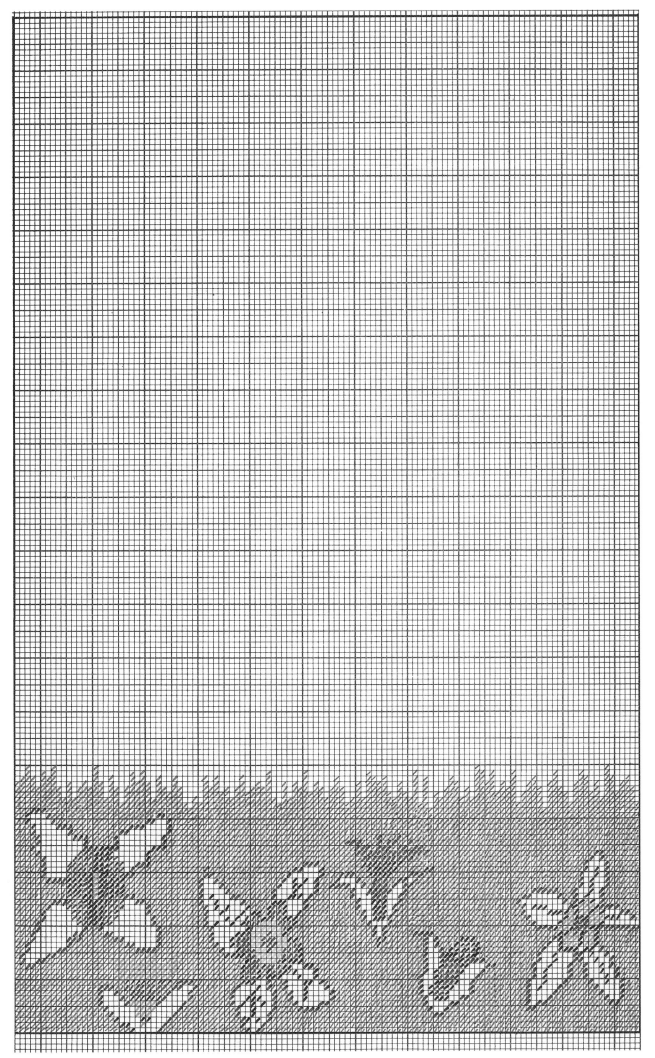

Rabbit with Flowers
Crew-Neck Pullover

RABBIT WITH FLOWERS CREW-NECK PULLOVER

A wonderful rendition of a loveable bunny hopping right out of his framed boundary into a field of pink flowers. He's a BIG hit wherever he goes. On an off-white ground with pink and green flowers, he can be knit as a white and black fluffy rabbit in mohair with a wool background, or grey and black cotton on a cotton background. Flowers are knit as entire circles filled in, or for an open and airy look, leave the center white and make circles with the pink. No matter which you choose, he'll fast become a favorite.

MATERIALS: 20 oz. off-white wool or cotton in sport weight, or yarn to give gauge below. 3 oz. each of reddish-pink and dark green. 1 oz. light green, 150 yards of mohair for the rabbit in white, and 50 yards in black.

NEEDLES: Size 4 and 6. One set of double-point needles size 4.

GAUGE: 5½ sts = 1 inch. 7 rows = 1 inch.

SIZE: These directions are for a size 40″ finished garment. Measurements are: length to underarm 13″, length to shoulder 22″, length of sleeve to underarm 17″.

To alter size, see instructions for SIZING.

NOTE: Do *NOT* carry yarn across. Use a new yarn for each color change and twist old and new yarns around each other to prevent holes.

SPECIAL NOTE: This sweater can also be knit as a large, oversize sweater using worsted weight wool and size 8 or 7 needles. Finished garment on size 8 needles is: width 48″, length 25½″. Sweater worked on size 7 needles will give measurements of: width 44″, length 24″. Materials needed will be slightly more than those listed above.

FRONT: With smaller needles cast on 98 sts and work in K1, P1, ribbing for 3 inches. Change to larger needles and increase 12 sts evenly spaced across next row in st st. Continue in st st and work charted pattern, binding off and decreasing as indicated. Place center 14 sts on holder for neck ribbing.

BACK: Work back to match front, omitting bunny pattern and working flowers over entire back. Place center 38 sts on holder for neck ribbing.

SLEEVES: With smaller needles, cast on 40 sts and work in K1, P1, ribbing for 3 inches. Change to larger needles and working in st st increase 36 sts evenly spaced in next row. Work sleeves according to charted design and bind off loosely.

Sew shoulder seams.

NECK: With double-point needles, pick up a total of 104 sts, including sts from front and back holders. Work in K1, P1, ribbing for 1 inch. Bind off loosely in ribbing.

Sew sleeves in place. Sew underarm and sleeve seams. Weave in loose threads.

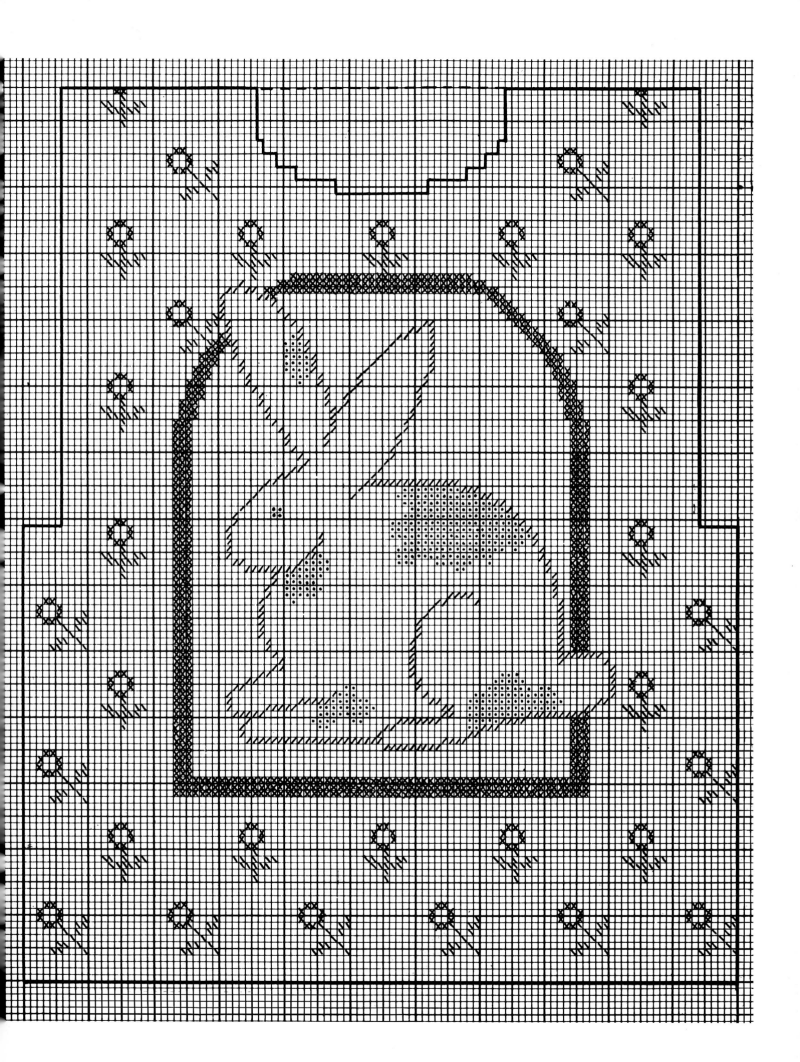

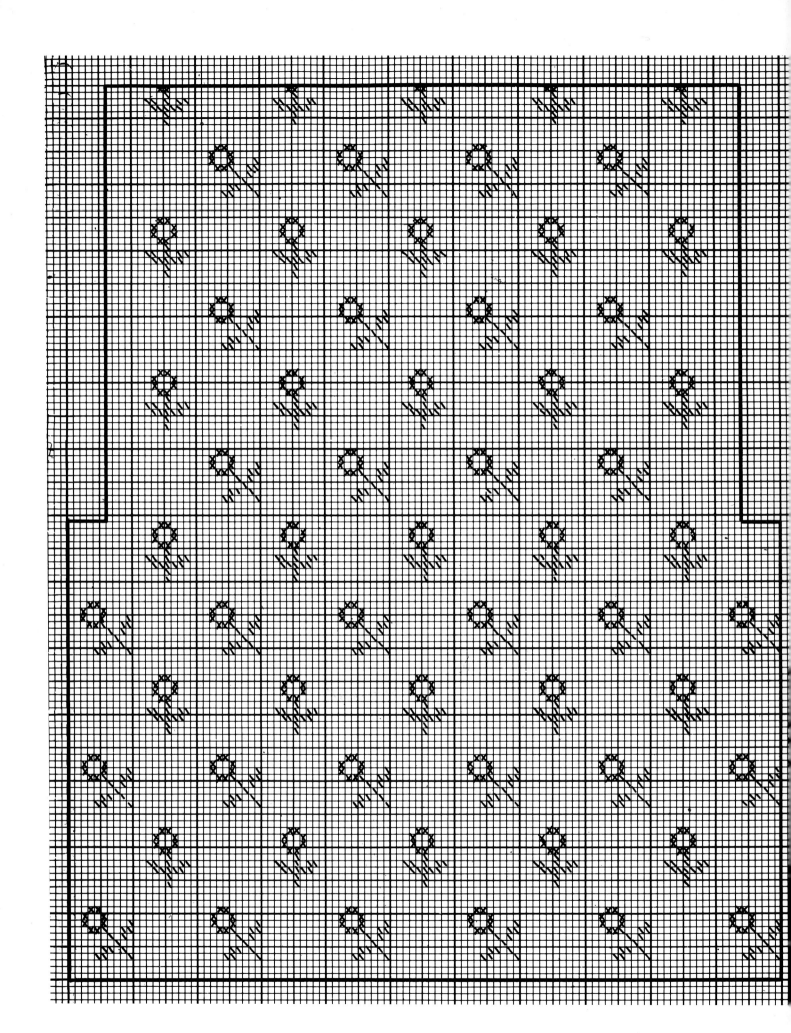

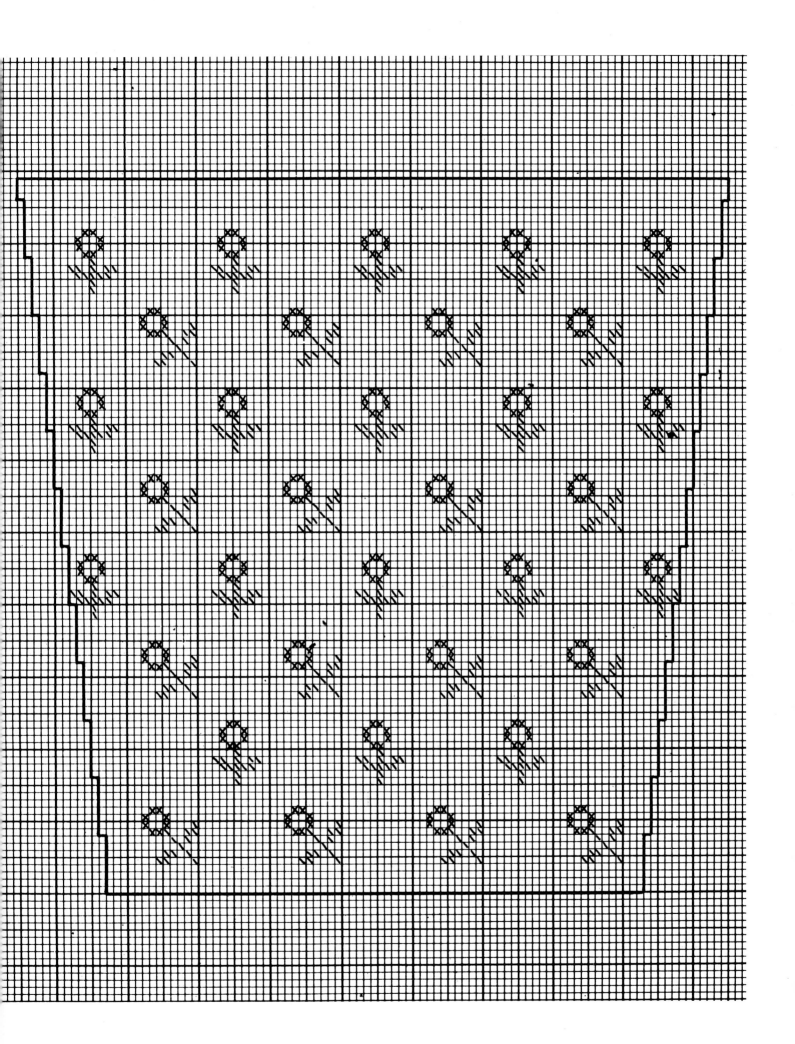

YARN MANUFACTURERS IN THE U.S.

If you have trouble finding the yarns you would like to use, contact these manufacturers for a list of the dealers nearest you.

ANDEAN YARNS
54 Industrial Way
Wilmington, Mass. 01887
(617) 657-7680
$3.00/color cards

ARMEN CORP.
(Chat Botte)
1400 Brevard Rd.
Asheville, N.C. 28806
(704) 667-9902

ARMOUR HANDCRAFTS INC.
(Bucilla)
150 Meadowland Pkwy.
Secaucus, N.J. 07094
(201) 330-9100

BERNAT YARN & CRAFT CORP.
Depot & Mendon Sts.
Uxbridge, Mass. 01569
(617) 278-2414

BOUQUET YARNS USA
51 Covert Ave.
Floral Park, N.Y. 11001
(516) 354-8537

BRUNSWICK WORSTED MILLS INC.
Brunswick Ave.
Moosup, Conn. 06354
(203) 564-2761

BUCILLA
(3 Suisses)
230 Fifth Ave.
New York, N.Y. 10021

CANDIDE YARNS
Woodbury, Conn. 06796

CASWELL SHEEP & WOOL CO.
Rt. 1, Box 135
Blanch, N.C. 27212
(919) 694-4838

CIRCULO YARNS INC.
(cotton)
7963 N.W. 14th St.
Miami, Fla. 33126
(305) 594-0404

COLUMBIA-MINERVA
230 Fifth Ave.
New York, N.Y. 10001
(212) 685-2907

CONSHOHOCKEN COTTON CO.
Ford Bridge Rd.
Conshohocken, Pa. 19428
(215) 825-4270

CRYSTAL PALACE YARNS
3006 San Pablo Ave.
Berkeley, Calif. 94702
(415) 548-9988

DYED IN THE WOOL, LTD.
252 W. 37th St.
New York, N.Y. 10018
(212) 563-6669

E'LITE SPECIALTY YARNS INC.
750 Suffolk St.
Lowell, Mass. 01854
(617) 453-2837

ERDOL YARNS LTD.
(designer yarns)
303 5th Ave.
Room 1109
New York, N.Y. 10016
(212) 725-0162
$5/color card

FAIR DINKUM IMPORTS
7525 Harold Ave.
Golden Valley, Minn. 55427
(612) 545-6471

FANTACIA, INC.
(distributor for Lana Gatto)
415 E. Beach Ave.
Inglewood, Calif. 90302
(213) 673-7914

JOSEPH GALLER
27 West 20th St.
New York, N.Y. 10011

GRANDOR INDUSTRIES, LTD.
(Sunbeam)
4031 Knobhill Drive
Sherman Oaks, Calif. 91403

HERRSCHNERS
999 Plaza Drive
Suite 660
Schaumburg, Ill. 60195
(312) 843-6931

S. & C. HUBER, AMERICAN CLASSICS
82 Plants Dam Road
East Lyme, Conn. 06333
(203) 739-0772
$3/color card

KENDEX CORP.
(Sirdar)
31332 Via Colinas #107
Westlake Village, Calif. 91362

KIWI IMPORTS, INC.
(Perendale)
54 Industrial Way
Wilmington, Mass. 01887
(617) 657-8566
(617) 938-0077

LAINES ANNY BLATT
24770 Crestview Ct.
Farmington Hills, Mich. 48018
(313) 474-2942

LION BRAND YARN CO.
1270 Broadway
New York, N.Y. 10001
(212) 736-7937

MERINO WOOL INC.
(Emu and Picaud)
230 Fifth Ave.
20th Floor
New York, N.Y. 10001

NOMOTTA YARNS, INC.
60 E. 42nd St. #3421
New York, N.Y. 10165
(212) 687-3361
(516) 933-0994

PHILDAR
6438 Dawson Boulevard
85 North
Norcross, Ga. 30093

PHILIPS IMPORTS
(Sunbeam)
P.O. Box 146
Port St. Joe, Fla. 32456

PINGOUIN-PROMAFIL CORP.
P.O. Box 100
Highway 45
Jamestown, S.C. 29453

REYNOLDS YARN INC.
15 Oser Ave.
Hauppauge, N.Y. 11788
(516) 582-9330

SCHAFFHAUSER
938 NW Couch
Portland, Ore. 97209
(503) 222-3022

SCHEEPJESWOL USA INC.
155 Lafayette Ave.
North White Plains, N.Y. 10603
(800) 431-4040; in N.Y. (914) 997-8

SHEPHERD WOOLS INC.
917 Industry Dr.
Seattle, Wash. 98188
(206) 575-0131

SUGAR RIVER YARNS
P.O. Box 663
New Glarus, Wis. 53574

TAHKI IMPORTS LTD.
92 Kennedy St.
Hackensack, N.J. 07601
(201) 489-9505

ULTEX
21 Adley Rd.
Cambridge, Mass. 02138
(800) 343-5080
(617) 491-6744

WILLIAM UNGER
230 Fifth Ave.
New York, N.Y. 10001
(212) 532-0689

WENDY YARNS U.S.A.
P.O. Box 11672
Milwaukee, Wis. 53211

YARN MANUFACTURERS IN THE U.K. AND FRANCE

CHAT BOTTE
BP 34959056
Roubaix
Cedex 1
France

EMU WOOLS
Leeds Road
Greengates
Bradford
West Yorks
U.K.

HAYFIELD MILLS
Glusburn
Nr. Keighley
West Yorks BD20 8QP
U.K.

LISTER-LEE
George Lee & Sons Ltd.
White Oak Mills
P.O. Box 37
Wakefield
West Yorks
U.K.

PHILDAR
4 Gambrel Road
Westgate Industrial Estate
Northampton NN5 5NS
U.K.

SIRDAR LTD.
Flanshaw Lane
Alverthorpe
Wakefield WF2 9ND
U.K.

SUNBEAM
Richard Ingram & Co. Ltd.
Cranshaw Mills
Pudsey LS28 7BS
U.K.

3 SUISSES
Marlborough House
38 Welford Road
Leicester LE2 7AA
U.K.

WENDY INTERNATIONAL
P.O. Box 3
Guiseley
West Yorks
U.K.